ANATOMY OF A BLACK MOTHER

JANELLE WOOD

CONTENTS

—

*I dedicate this book to all of the mothers
of Black children whose children deserve
to be educated, heard, and valued.*

ACKNOWLEDGEMENTS

The thought of writing a book was challenging to me, and without my Lord and Savior, Jesus Christ, and the support of my family and friends, *Anatomy of a Black Mother* would not have been birthed.

I would be remiss if I did not acknowledge my family: my loving husband, Andrew, who is my rock and continues to love me graciously and patiently while I am out serving in our community; and my beloved son, Bryce Michael, for without him, I would have never known the joys, heartaches, and courage it takes to be a Black mother of a Black son in America.

To my grandma, my mother, Barbara, dad, sisters, stepparents, and extended family, thank you so very much for always being there for me. Thanks to the amazing Black Mothers Forum team who have served alongside of me in this work to dismantle the school to prison pipeline and create safe and supportive learning environments for our Black children. Thank you to the Adam Colwell's WriteWorks, LLC team.

Finally, I thank all of the allies and Black mothers along the way who allowed me to advocate on behalf of their children and for all of my beautiful Black daughters and sons. I love you all, and I am grateful that you gave me permission to walk out this thing called life with you.

FOREWORD

Parent, activist, author of Voices, Choices, and Second Chances *and* School Choice: A Legacy to Keep, *and subject of the motion picture,* Miss Virginia
~ Virginia Walden Ford

In my very first conversation with Janelle Wood, I felt tremendously uplifted and excited. I had been truly worried about the chaos in our world. Hearing Janelle's personal story, and learning about her work with Black Mothers Forum, gave me hope for changes in the future.

Anatomy of a Black Mother will grab you as you share in Janelle's journey, and the journeys of many Black mothers, in understanding and accepting their role in the fight for their children and families in today's society.

Systemic racism is rooted deeply in America, and, therefore, cannot easily be corrected. For many of us who have spent a lifetime fighting for racial justice, this is a moment of reckoning that has eluded us for far too long. As James Baldwin wrote in *The Cross of Redemption: Uncollected Writings*, "Not everything that is faced can be changed, but nothing can be changed until it is faced."

Therefore, I believe that for any change to occur, it absolutely must be faced. Janelle has certainly "faced it" and brought so many mothers along with her.

I have been fighting for justice for a long time. When we were fighting for educational opportunities for the young people of Washington, D.C., people tried to divide us. Well, first they tried to dismiss us, and when they could not do that, they tried to defeat us, and when they could not do that, then they tried to divide us.

In the pages of this book, you will get to know Janelle and the many mothers who are fighting for their children, their families, and their communities. THEY WILL NOT BE DIVIDED.

I pray that you will, as I have, feel the energy in these pages and share it with those around you.

Virginia Walden Ford
www.virginiawaldenford.com
www.missvirginiamovie.com

NOTE FROM THE AUTHOR

The events and accounts depicted in this book are related as best as I remember them, and they have been researched as thoroughly as possible to ensure accuracy. In many cases, I chose not to use an individual's actual name to protect their identity. I also did my best to not misrepresent any person or incident in any way.

—

BLACK MOTHERS ARISE!

"Start children off on the way they should go,
and even when they are old they will not turn from it."
~ Proverbs 22:6

For you to understand how I became founder, in 2016, of Black Mothers Forum, Inc.—a non-profit organization dedicated to ending the bloodshed in the Black community, dismantling the school to prison pipeline, and restoring the strength, dignity, and hope of the Black community—I have to take you back to the beginning.

It was when I first became a Black mother myself that I started a journey of understanding that what goes on inside of the heart of a mother is going to be transferred to her child. Our children are the joy of our lives, and we want to see them have every opportunity to be successful and become all that God created them to be.

We'll do whatever it takes to make that happen.

Yet our habits, traditions, fears, and how we view ourselves are all projected onto our children, and they are going to project that in their lives in the way they make decisions and respond to particular situations.

My only child, Bryce, became almost a full-time job because I wanted to make sure he stayed in school, didn't get into any trouble with the police, and was able to explore who he was safely at school and elsewhere. But I started running into roadblocks early on when the school psychologist evaluated Bryce in third grade and reported that he should be put on Ritalin, a stimulant used to treat attention deficit hyperactivity disorder (ADHD). The report said my son was unfocused, could not settle down in class, and was a behavior problem. At that time, raising my son with his father, I didn't recognize what was going on. In fact, in my naivete, I thought I was the only one going through something like this.

It wasn't unusual for me to have to leave work and go to the school to talk to my son, the teachers, and the principal just so they wouldn't suspend him, even though he wasn't a bad kid. That's what they kept saying. "He's not bad. He's not getting in trouble *that* way. He talks too much, and he is distracted in class."

I hated that. The bottom line was that he was entertaining the class. Little did I know then that he was going to grow up to become a professional actor. What he was doing was exploring and expressing his natural, authentic self, and he was being penalized for it. I felt my son was unable to be himself and was not being given the freedom to learn to manage his behavior the same way his White peers were. I saw it as an injustice that my son could not just be a third grader, but instead he was expected to behave like an adult version of himself.

We submitted the school psychologist's report to our son's Black pediatrician who refuted the findings and concluded instead that our son was simply bored and needed to be challenged. He recommended Bryce be tested for the school's gifted program. Lo and behold, he passed the test and was transferred into the gifted program. Bryce did not have any more problems keeping himself focused because he was finally being challenged. He was never diagnosed with either ADHD or attention deficit disorder (ADD).

Still, from grade school, through middle school, and into high school, administrators and teachers continued to try and label my son as being somewhat disruptive. It became clear to us that our son thrived much better when he had a set routine and was being challenged throughout his day. Bryce just needed to have space to be creative so that he could succeed.

While we were going through all of this, my husband and I had not yet identified that Bryce also needed to be placed in extracurricular activities that afforded him the opportunity to perform. Nevertheless, we ended up allowing him to pursue his interests in singing in school ensembles, acting in plays, and taking drama classes. We also kept him active in sports, starting with club basketball, football, and track in his earlier years. When he was older, Bryce played football and ran track for his schools. There were still times Bryce would get off task, like when he missed tutoring during his school lunch hours because he decided that he needed to entertain his friends and classmates, but I was blessed to have a job where I could leave at any time to help redirect his activities and make sure *he* was where he was supposed to be.

Often, I had to meet with teachers and school administrators to make certain Bryce was not labelled, reassuring them that my husband and I were very much present in our son's academic and personal life and were willing to do our part to ensure he had a rewarding educational experience.

There was an incident in middle school where my son was accused of possessing and accessing pornography. This happened for two reasons. First, a little girl who liked Bryce created and gave him a pictorial collage of music artist, Beyonce. He displayed it in his locker, and school officials alleged he was promoting soft pornography. Second, two of Bryce's White male peers used his school password to look up actual pornography on his school computer. They were never questioned, even after my son specified that they used his password without his knowledge or permission. When Bryce tried to explain these incidents to the vice principal, a White female, she dismissed him—then called and told me he was about to be suspended and labelled as a sex offender.

I immediately expressed my total disagreement with this course of action, but it became clear to me that the vice principal was still intent on placing the offensive infraction in my son's discipline record. When my husband and I realized our son's school was setting him up to be labelled as a sex offender, we moved him to another school. Our whole goal was to make sure our son felt safe and supported in his learning environment. The school we placed him in had a more diverse environment and a Black male principal. The documentation the vice principal planned to place into Bryce's discipline record never made it into his file.

Beyond his elementary school years, and after Bryce was identified as a gifted student, we admitted him into the International

Baccalaureate program. Bryce was usually around students who were challenged to be academically excellent—but the same could not be said for many of his Black and Hispanic peers. I began setting the stage back then for what I'm doing now without even realizing it by advocating for the academic well-being of other children.

I'd ask administrators, "How come you set the bar so low for the other students in this school, and yet students who are in the International Baccalaureate program have the bar set so high? How come my son's peers don't have the bar set high for them as well?"

"Ms. Wood," they responded, "these kid's parents just have them going to school because it is required. These kids probably won't amount to much because, if you look at their parents, they are not doing all that well. This is a gang area. Most of these kids will probably go on and become gang members. But your child will be different because you poured so much into him." Then they added, "I don't know why you are so concerned about these other kids."

I couldn't believe what I was hearing, and I was insulted on behalf of the other parents. "The reason I am concerned," I countered, "is that these are my son's peers. This is the group of people he will grow up with and do life with, and you ask me why I'm concerned? If you are pouring all of this into my son and not into his peers, it is setting him apart and making it seem as if he is better than others. We have also taught Bryce to never think that he is better than anyone else. We all deserve to be our best selves if given the opportunity. We taught him to be a team player."

I was angry, and I pushed it as far as I could. I went all the way to the superintendent, but all I got was the same old song and dance. "Ms. Wood, your son is going to make it because of who you are. But those other kids are just meeting a requirement. They are only in school because they are required by law to be there, but they will probably end up in gangs, on drugs, in prison, or dead."

To hear educators say that and take that overall view about certain kids really bothered me.

It would stay with me for years.

Fast forward to 2022. Bryce had successfully completed a Bachelor of Arts degree in Film, Theater, and Television from the University of Notre Dame and a Master of Arts degree in Performing Arts with an emphasis in acting from the University of Connecticut. Bryce has secured many acting opportunities since he graduated with his masters in 2018. My husband and I wanted to make sure Bryce grew up in a stable environment that allowed him to fully express himself, with boundaries, while creating the structures he needed to be successful. We made it a point to walk him through how to properly make life decisions: pray first, seek godly counsel, identify role models, and request their assistance. Bryce incorporated all he was taught, and he has set himself up on a daily schedule of praying, devotional time, setting his tasks for the day, cooking meals ahead of time, and going over his lines for auditions or roles. He is stable and independent. We are so very proud of him.

In August 1989, two years before Bryce was born, I received my Bachelor of Arts degree in economics from Arizona State University (ASU). Raised in a Christian home, I rededicated my life to God in 1996 when Bryce was around five years of age, and I was called by God to go into the ministry three years later. While

Bryce was in elementary and middle school, I went to Phoenix Seminary from 2000-2005 and received my Master of Arts in Biblical Leadership. I truly believed God was calling me to become a church Sunday School administrator.

I did just that at first, but then God moved on me to become a minister. I secured a position as the executive assistant for Reverend Braxton Moore at one of Phoenix's largest Black churches. That also led to me being licensed and ordained as the First Daughter of the church. In Rev. Moore's years prior to that, he had never considered licensing a woman as a minister in his church. Rev. Moore didn't believe women should be preachers. Many other women had come before me, and he had refused each one. It was Rev. Moore who first brought up the idea of me becoming a licensed minister. I looked at him like he was crazy, but the Lord finally moved on me to pursue a life in ministry, and after much prayer, I accepted the assignment.

I worked with Rev. Moore for one-and-a-half years before the Lord changed things up once again and put me to work in city government in 2004. I didn't understand that at all. I wondered why I had to be chief of staff for one of the city councilmembers. I came on board during the last half of his first term in office and remained through the first half of his second term, about four years in all. Though I struggled with why I was there instead of in Christian ministry, I learned a lot about city, state, and federal government, knowledge that is proving essential to me today.

While I worked in city government, I also began serving the homeless in 2005 through First Watch Ministries, an organization the Lord laid on my heart to start so I could share the gospel of Jesus Christ with those who found themselves uncomfortable with being in a church building. I had never done work with the homeless community, but I discovered God had chosen me to share His love with prostitutes, veterans, drug dealers, substance abusers, ex-felons, runaway teenagers, and whoever else found their way to us. Through my position in city government, I was able to advocate for greater access to housing, jobs, mental health counseling services, and substance abuse services for our homeless church members and any of the others who came for help.

When I asked the Lord to show me why He had set me apart for this work, He clearly said, "You are the voice for those without a voice."

That was the first time I'd heard Him say those words to me.

Then God surprised me yet again, calling me to serve with a women's biblical leadership organization. Shortly thereafter, I prepared for the first of six short-term mission trips to the Middle East starting in 2010, the same year Bryce graduated from high school. Next thing I knew, I was in Turkey working with Arab women to help them understand the Bible, develop their own ministries, and help them with their own character development. On every trip, the Lord prompted me to look and *see* everything around me—especially what was happening in the lives of the women we were serving. I did not specifically know why He wanted me to do that, but I did as He directed.

I watched, and I remembered.

I did that for approximately four years before ending those short-term missionary trips and returning home to Arizona in 2014. I started volunteering with a local prison ministry as a pastor and then overseer at the women's prison located west of Phoenix in Goodyear, Arizona.

I was one of the worship services pastors, and I was responsible for coordinating praise and worship music, service order, delivering a sermon, and praying over any woman who needed or requested it. As I facilitated worship services and met the women, I began to realize I wasn't seeing a lot of Black women in attendance. I thought that was odd. I certainly saw many Black women when I walked through the prison yard to get to the room where we conducted our worship services. At the time I showed up, usually around 5:30 p.m., whatever they had been doing that day was pretty much over, so they had recreational time. I saw the women getting their exercise by walking around the track and playing basketball, or just sitting on benches talking with one another.

Whenever I walked onto a prison yard, all I could see was bars. I heard the big metal iron gates close behind me as I moved from one entrance to another. They took my badge and checked their computer each time to make sure I was still cleared as a volunteer to conduct worship services. I went to six different prison yards within the women's prison complex each month. I felt the bondage that each one of our women in prison have had to endure daily for years. Each yard had its own level of security depending on the crimes the women were convicted of, anywhere from minimum to medium security yards. A different minister was assigned to the maximum security yard.

Being a volunteer, I was not allowed to interact with the women when they were outside. Inside, they had to sit several feet away from me. I couldn't touch them or hug them. I had to make sure I kept them at a distance because they didn't want anyone to get close enough to possibly shank me, and they didn't want us close enough to them to slip notes back and forth. They also limited the resources we could bring in and hand out. When we distributed music books, they had to be returned. We couldn't give them anything with loose leaf pages. Everything had to be stapled, and each booklet had to be checked before we left. Guards stood behind the ladies to watch for any suspicious behavior during the worship services.

One evening, I had just finished a service at one of the minimum security yards. As I was collecting the music books, one of the older Black women who had regularly attended my worship services pulled me aside as she helped me gather our music books. There were guards in the room, but it was a more relaxed setting where the women were allowed to approach and talk to me. This particular woman and I had developed a nice rapport over time.

"I bet you wonder why you don't see many of us here in your worship services," she said.

"I do," I replied, "because I know most Black people have gone to church, or at least were raised in church, and this would be an opportunity for them to be uplifted and receive some spiritual nourishment."

She leaned in and whispered, "You know, we have to get permission to come to church."

I must have had this look on my face that said, "What?"

Then she said, "Look on the wall. What do you see?"

I looked at the wall to my left. In the photographs were the chaplains who currently worked at the women's prison: White male chaplains.

"Isn't it interesting," she said, "that we don't get permission to come to worship service?"

Then she had me look across the way through a big window, where I saw a long line of Black women in front of the infirmary where they were getting medications like antidepressants, Prozac, and so on.

She looked down and stated, "They would much rather drug us than allow us to get spiritually fed."

Another lady, a younger Black girl, was standing nearby.

"That is why so many of us come out addicted to drugs," she added quietly. "Many of us who were not addicted to drugs become addicted while we are in here because they put us on these drugs." She then explained that when fellow inmates were released, they'd get picked back up on a drug offense and end up returning to prison because they had to find a way to take care of the addiction that they developed during their time in prison.

> That is recidivism—and it relentlessly feeds off of people of color.

I started to understand that was what kept the system going. It perpetuated repeat offenses so released inmates kept coming back, and the prison system kept making money off of them.

That is recidivism. It's a vicious cycle that has been around longer than most people realize—and it relentlessly feeds off of people of color, especially our Black sons and daughters.

It was then that the Lord began moving on my heart to work with Black women, and more specifically, Black mothers. God's Holy Spirit said, "I need you to meet with Black mothers."

Initially, that was all I got—but I also recalled how the Lord had often prompted me in the Middle East to watch and remember what was going on in the women's lives there. That caused me to think, too, about what I had started seeing more and more on the television news. Black mothers pouring out their hearts after their unarmed Black sons had been shot and killed by the police. At that time, the death of Michael Brown, Jr. was the latest incident in August 2014. But there had been others before him that same year. Tyree Woodson, suspected of killing himself in the bathroom of the police station after being arrested, also in August. Eric Garner, who died in a police chokehold, in July. Dontre Hamilton, who was shot by a police officer while unarmed, in April.

Still, I questioned Him. "Really? Why do I need to meet with Black mothers?"

He gave me only the detail I needed at the time. "I *need* you to meet with Black mothers. I am going to *use* the mothers."

After that, whenever I prayed for God to show me how He was going to use them, I received no answer.

Near the end of 2014, the Lord led me to talk with Nina Thomas. We'd known each other from the time I served under Rev. Moore. She was an executive assistant for another pastor in the same neighborhood. We'd become good friends, but I hadn't seen or heard from her in quite some time, and I didn't know how to get in touch with her.

But the Lord was clear. He said Nina would be able to tell me what the Black mothers were supposed to do.

Then an email from her popped up in my inbox. I was on a group email Nina sent out about the job she was doing at the university. It said she had become an assistant associate director for a department focused on the study of race and democracy. I responded to confirm I had received her email, and then I shared with her how God had laid it on my heart that I was supposed to talk to her about some things He'd dropped in my spirit, and that she would know what I was supposed to do.

She replied, "Let's do what God said."

I asked her to meet me for lunch in early December 2014. I sat across from Nina, a woman I hadn't seen for years, and told her again about how God had told me I was supposed to do something with Black mothers. "Problem is," I said, "I don't know what I am supposed to do with them."

"I don't know either," she responded, "but let's eat."

We did, and we spent time catching up on each other's lives since we had worked with our respective churches. We had pretty much completed our lunch when Nina looked up from her plate.

"I think I know what you are supposed to do. You need to attend my book club meeting."

It wasn't exactly the answer I was expecting—but she explained that it started that Saturday at a local church and that they would be discussing *The New Jim Crow* by Michelle Alexander. It was all about the mass incarceration of Black people.

"I don't know how it ties to Black mothers," Nina admitted, "but the Lord has definitely told me you need to do that book study."

I was obedient. I ordered the book, and I showed up for the book study every month while I was still volunteering at the women's prison.

It was nothing short of amazing.

As we read and discussed the book, I started to gain a better understanding of what I witnessed when I went to the women's prison to conduct my worship services. I recognized the disproportionate treatment of Black women in prison versus how White women were being treated. I saw the difference in opportunities and access to various privileges that White women inmates had over Black women inmates, not just for spiritual programs like my worship services, but for prison work opportunities, the dispensing of toiletries, and the number of visits allowed for family members. No reasons were given. The White women simply had more privileges.

As I started to connect some things, I knew something wasn't right.

In *The New Jim Crow*, Michelle described the school to prison pipeline—the conduit used since the 1980s to criminalize the normal childlike behaviors of our Black children, often through harsh, lengthy, and punitive disciplinary measures such as school suspensions and expulsions for minor infractions such as disrespect, attitudes, questioning the teacher, and so on. When children are removed from school, they get behind in their coursework. They start to lose interest and become discouraged. Then, because they are usually left home alone while their parents are at work, they find themselves in situations that increase their chances of coming into contact with law enforcement.

Those encounters often result in either imprisonment or death.

What she wrote resonated with my heart.

It also made my heart break over what our Black children had been going through for decades.

As I made these sobering and frightening discoveries in Michelle's book, I still didn't think back to Bryce's school experiences—not yet anyway. While I was still reading and learning, I was also thinking, *Okay, Lord, thank you for showing me this while I am going into the prisons, but I still don't know why I am supposed to meet with Black mothers. Why can't I go meet with everybody in the community? This is a community problem.*

It still hadn't clicked, and it would take me a while longer before I finally got it.

We ended the study in December 2015, at which point our book club leader decided we would take a break and then return in January to decide what to do. In her book, Michelle closes with directives and calls-to-action, asking readers to take the information and educate those around them, push for prison reform, run for office, or organize protests. Our group was under the impression that, since we were holding our meetings in a church, we would roll out the information to the church first, maybe in Sunday School classes or to the men's, women's, or youth groups, before doing presentations to the full congregation. We figured someone from the church would then take charge and proceed from there.

January 2016 arrived and passed, and the wife of the gentleman who was leading the book club passed away. Meanwhile, I was working full time in management with an insurance company. In March, Mary Johnson, a mother who had recently recovered from breast cancer for the third time, called me at work, asking me what we should do with the information we had just learned. As a member of the book study, she was aware of how the Lord was leading me to meet with Black mothers because I had mentioned it a few times during our book discussions.

"So, what are you going to do about that?" she asked.

"I don't know," I responded, a little confused. I continued to believe that what I had learned in the book study and God's prompting about the mothers were two different things.

Mary told me she had talked to the leader of the book study. He'd told her he was ready to call a meeting of the study group to discuss next steps. I told Mary to be sure to let him know that I wanted to be included in the meeting.

Another month passed before I heard from Mary again. She said the leader still hadn't met with anyone, and that we needed to do something. She also asked me again about the Black mothers, and I told her I still didn't know.

Then in May, Mary called again—and she was somewhat irritated with me.

"Now, look," she challenged. "You are supposed to be doing something, and you need to get on it!"

Taken aback, I asked about the leader of the book study. She said there had been a meeting, but she found out about it too late to let me know. "He just wants to start the book all over again," she reported, obviously annoyed.

I couldn't believe it. "Excuse me?"

"I said exactly the same thing," Mary replied. "He said he didn't think we fully understood what to do and that we should read it again." She paused to catch her breath. "Janelle, you have to do something. I *know* you are supposed to do something. You need to get with the churches in your area and talk to some of the pastors."

Then she added, "What about those Black mothers? If you don't want to do what God has called you to do, He will give it to someone else."

That did it.

I ended the call with Mary. "All right, Lord." I said aloud. "What do you want me to do with these Black mothers? Talk to me."

God said, "I need you to meet with them. Set up the meeting."

Well, I hemmed and hawed and didn't do anything. As June came and went, I felt I was getting a clearer directive as the Lord reopened my eyes and ears to see and hear the cries of Black mothers on TV who were wringing their hands and crying in the street over the fatal shootings of their unarmed Black sons. I sensed the Lord saying to me at that time, "It is time," yet I waited. In early July, the Lord moved on me again, unmistakably emphasizing that it was *now* time to meet with the Black mothers.

> The Black mothers are crying about losing their children.

"What are we going to meet about?" I asked.

I could almost see the Lord shaking His head. "Look around. Don't you see what I've shown you before? The Black mothers are crying about losing their children."

There it was.

Suddenly, it clicked. I put it all together—from my experiences with Bryce, to the women I served in the Middle East, to the ones I ministered to prison, and the ones I saw on TV.

"I need you to bring them together in your community to address what is happening," God said. "They need a voice. *You* are that voice for those without a voice."

They were the same words God had first spoken to me a decade earlier when I began working with the homeless. The Lord was showing me that we had another community without a voice: our Black mothers wailing over the loss of their Black children. Exactly who I would be speaking to on behalf of the mothers wasn't clear yet, but I knew I was going to be the one to help articulate their pain and their needs to those in authority. I also understood that I was supposed to take what they told me and create a statement that spoke to their pain and to what they wanted done to resolve that pain.

I created a flyer and sent it out to all the women I knew. I had compiled a pretty wide network of Black mothers by then, dating from the time I served in city government. I also knew parents from when Bryce was in school. I sent out a detailed email inviting everyone to what I called a "Black mothers forum." It had taken a couple of weeks to find a venue, but I had finally nailed one down: a library in the heart of our community.

The meeting was scheduled for the afternoon of August 7, 2016.

At first, no one except Mary responded to my email. Approximately one week later, another mother, Nancy Cooper, who was part of the book study, said she would come. Then Nina said she'd be there. *Alright,* I thought. *That'll be enough. We'll get started.*

A week-and-a-half before the meeting, a murder occurred. It was a police shooting in Tempe, Arizona where a 19-year-old Black man, Dalvin Hollins, was shot in the back by a Tempe police officer. According to reports from the *Arizona Republic,* police caught up with Dalvin, who was walking near a Walgreens that had just been robbed and was carrying a bag similar to the one drugstore workers said the robber had taken from the store. A chase ensued, with one officer on foot and the other pursuing in his police cruiser. That officer hopped out of his cruiser and was chasing Dalvin near a senior living center when he fired one round, striking Dalvin in the back.

Circumstances surrounding the incident led to several community protests, including one rally that led to three arrests after protesters briefly shut down the Mill Avenue bridge. The protesters were tear gassed. It was a big deal. It was all over the television news.

A town hall meeting about the shooting was called one week before the meeting I had called with Black mothers. I was unaware of the town hall meeting, but Nina went. I was not invited to attend. The day after the town hall, Nina called me. "I'm so glad you called your meeting," she said. "You should have a lot more mothers show up because one of the larger Black churches had a lot of Black mothers show up at the town hall, only to be silenced."

Nina then explained that each one of the church's leaders got up and gave a mini sermon when everyone was instead expecting to be told what they were going to do as a community about the killing of their unarmed children by the police. "All these women lined up at the different mics to talk, and in essence the pastor got up and said, 'I need all y'all to sit down. Let's hear from the media first. We will hear from y'all after they get a chance to ask their questions.'" Nina said that set off a ruckus, and the minister lost control of the meeting. "The Black mothers took over," she said, "and they let everybody have it."

I had approximately 40 Black mothers show up August 7—and they were hot and ready to set it off. All I did was stand up and say, "Welcome. I'm glad you're here. This is a place where we meet, and if you want to cry it out, cuss it out, whatever you want to do—this is our space and our time to talk about what's in our hearts and what we need to do about it."

Each mother got up one by one and shared her heart, concerns, anger, rage, fear—everything. The next two hours were full of tears and emotion. They needed to get it out.

After they all shared, I asked if they wanted to do it again.

They most certainly did.

We agreed to meet monthly on the second Sunday at 2:30 p.m.—and we have been meeting ever since. They wanted to get organized right away, too, so I asked questions and each meeting built on the previous one. After our first three meetings, the mothers wanted to set up a corporation and a nonprofit. I asked them to identify the top three urgent issues facing the Black community. We broke up into groups to talk about it, brainstormed, and came to an agreement. They were:

1) Protect our Black sons now (most of the mothers there had sons).
2) Deal with systemic racism.
3) Deal with the post-traumatic stress disorder (PTSD) in the Black community.

Then one mother stood up. "We can't deal with any of that until we have prayer. I think we need to have a prayer team or a prayer focus."

So, we formed four subcommittees to address those four areas—the three urgent issues and prayer—and chose four women to be team leaders for each one of those areas. The teams were tasked to do research on each one of their assigned areas and report their findings at our monthly meetings so we could be educated.

I was given the responsibility to bring in experts to address the different areas. Nina spoke and gave us a history of racism, then Angelina Sanchez, a program manager for the university, facilitated a conversation on racism in America and shared data on race-related police brutality. Both presentations were very informative, and the mothers decided to put together a mission statement to establish the focus of our work and to determine which areas of expertise were needed in order to help us gain the knowledge and tools necessary to address our most urgent issues. Today our mission reads: Educate, Organize and Take Action to fulfill our purpose of promoting healthy mindsets and relationships to end the school to prison pipeline.

The stage was set for what we did next.

It was time to meet with the police—if we could.

One of the mothers, Patricia Lindley, was the community affairs director for our local police department. She gave a presentation regarding how the police were hired and retained and the training they received, as well as the legal levels of force they were allowed to use as determined by the courts. As she shared details about the different levels of force, we recognized that many steps were being skipped and that they were going straight for their guns when dealing with our unarmed Black community. Levels of force were particularly being overridden when it came to our children. It was clear. Police officers were not even following their own policies on the use of force.

Patricia also explained that there were boards in place designed to hold the police accountable, but that there were no Black people serving on these boards because, as she put it, they could not get Black people to be on these boards. She challenged us to apply for three specific boards: the use of force board, the disciplinary review board, and the human relations commission.

Several mothers took her up on that—and I joined them, applying for the use of force board and the disciplinary review board in December 2016. About four months later, it dawned on me that I had not yet been contacted, so I reached out to the police department to check on the status of my application.

"What application?" the clerk replied.

I said I had submitted it in December, and that I had a receipt verifying they had received it.

"You know, Ms. Wood, we are reorganizing a lot of stuff right now, so it could have very well been lost. Can you resubmit it?"

I got another copy of the application, resubmitted it, and life went on.

I did not hear back about my applications for the use of force board or the disciplinary review board until January 2019.

Three years later.

The other mothers never heard back at all.

It was apparent to me that the reason Black mothers were not on many of our municipal boards was because there was no response to the applications, even though we had been told there were vacancies available. When we inquired about the lack of response to our mothers' applications, we were advised that the delays we were encountering were not the norm but were due in large part to a reorganization of all of their municipal boards. Unfortunately, even after that reorganization effort, our mothers still experienced a delayed response or no response at all. Nevertheless, we have been persistent, and by the start of 2021, three of us were serving on at least one those three police boards. I was on the use of force and disciplinary review boards. In addition, two of our mothers were serving on the human relations commission.

As we continued to hear about mothers' experiences with their children's schools and with the police, we invited experts to our monthly meetings to address our concerns, answer questions, and help us gain a better understanding of the systems in place. In December 2016, we had a former deputy superintendent of the state's education department, Dr. Carolyn Robbins, speak—and she really got the mothers thinking about how we needed to zero in on the school system first to address the school to prison pipeline.

In her presentation, she shared that the people with the power to change policies for the creation of more equitable solutions as they related to discipline were the local school boards. Not only did they have the authority, she said, but they were beholden to taxpayers because they held elected positions. She also shared that school boards were predominately made up of White people and that many of the meetings were not attended by Black parents.

I knew she was right. We didn't attend those meetings. How could we? They were usually held in the early evening when parents were getting off work to come home and care for their families. When dealing with single parents, there can be significant challenges for them to regularly attend school board meetings due to their work schedules, parental responsibilities, or both. So,

Dr. Robbins challenged us to start attending school board meetings in our respective districts.

We had accepted the challenge with the police.

We were also ready to accept the challenge with the school boards.

To discover which schools had the biggest problems, we needed some data—and we got it with the help of Antonio Camacho, the director of one of our civil rights organizations. Its primary focus was to gather data on discipline for children of color or children of marginalized communities. They did this to not only address the high rates of in-school suspension, out-of-school suspension, or expulsion, but also the high amount of enrollment barriers to immigrant families. We needed to prove that these barriers prevented parents from exercising their prerogative to move their children to a more safe and supportive learning environment.

Antonio was a great community organizer and mobilizer, and as I explained to him what the mothers were about to do, he helped me fully understand the data they were collecting on disproportionate disciplinary practices. Specifically, he provided statistics for one of the largest high school districts in our county. The data was overwhelming: Black students (especially males) were being suspended and expelled at a rate six to eight times higher than anyone else. The rate for Hispanic boys was nearly as great. That gave us a perfect starting point.

In January 2017, we put together a committee to research upcoming school board meeting times as well as to learn if anything had been on their agendas over the past six months that supported our Black children's needs.

We were unable to identify any agenda items focused on providing for the well-being of our Black children within that past year.

We weren't surprised—but we were about to shift their focus.

We attended our first school governing board meeting on February 2, 2017. The six mothers who were present at the meeting had never before attended a school board meeting, much less felt welcome to do so. None of us knew what to expect. I told them to come looking professional and serious and to bring a pen and notebook so that we could take notes.

"What are we taking notes about?" one of them asked.

"It doesn't matter. The school board doesn't know that. Just listen, hear what they are saying, take notes, and don't crack a smile the whole time. Don't acknowledge anyone." I didn't want them to engage in conversation with anyone yet because we weren't fully informed. We needed to know what we were talking about before we could formulate what we needed to say.

We attended the school board meetings for a few months until I felt we were ready to address the governing board. I had continued to work with Antonio on how to extrapolate the data he provided in order for me to teach the mothers not only how to understand the data, but also how to articulate our concerns as it related to that data. By the September 2017 board meeting, our mothers were taking up a row and a half in the audience.

We crafted a statement addressing the disproportionality of disciplinary practices to give at the meeting. I knew that statement would then become part of the public record for that meeting. Attendees were each given three minutes to give a public comment, and I trained the mothers on how to detach their emotions from anything they said. "When we get emotional,"

I told them, "the board will lose sight of why we are here in the first place, and it gets personal. We need to stay factual."

I turned in my blue card to make my first public comment at the school district's regular governing board meeting on September 7, 2017. When I spoke, I read our foundational statement.

"We as Black mothers will no longer remain silent while our children are blatantly disrespected, provoked, threatened, neglected, and set up to fail through policies, curriculums, and disciplinary practices deeply rooted in racial stereotypes. We are requesting a study session of this district to address whether the policies, curriculums, and practices that are currently in place actually create a safe and supportive learning environment for our Black children, especially our Black sons. We want this study session to be placed on your agenda, and we want to be a part of the study session and the discussion. Thank you very much."

That was how we began.

None of the other mothers spoke that night—but in subsequent meetings, they did speak, making the same statement until the school board finally disclosed that they had already completed a districtwide study which showed the disproportionate disciplinary data we had requested. We worked with board member Richard Kensington to go over the disciplinary data they were able to extrapolate for all 21 of their high schools. Their study did indeed discover that their Black male students received the highest out-of-school suspensions of anyone on their school campuses. Richard committed to putting an equity resolution in place, and to working on other ways to create safe and supportive learning environments for their Black students.

As of March 2021, there had not been an equity and inclusion resolution set forth in the district policy, but their superintendent had made a commitment to create a more safe and supportive learning environment for their Black students through the implementation of restorative justice practices and listening groups for Black students and their families. The restorative justice program featured students participating in groups where they were able to freely express their feelings about a particular issue or situation while being held accountable for their actions by the group. It allowed both sides, the victims and the perpetrators, to take ownership of the conflict. The listening groups made it so Black students and their families could identify how to create the environments Black students needed in order to excel academically and socially.

Due to COVID-19 and the closure of the schools in 2020, most of that work had to be postponed. Much work remained to be done, and Black Mothers Forum was committed to make sure the high school district stayed the course once the schools reopened after the pandemic was over.

———

As word started to spread that we were requesting this type of data from school districts, parents began calling us about situations such as suspensions and expulsions being faced by their children. We also began hearing about how schools in the Phoenix metro area were presenting historical facts about the Black community in a discriminatory way, especially when dealing with the Civil War and slavery.

At a local elementary school, a fifth-grade class began with a game of Hangman on the board. The class included two Black girls and their predominantly White classmates. Their White male social studies teacher explained to the class that they were going to talk about slavery, and the best way he could think to do that was to play the game Hangman.

That sounds bad enough—but it got much worse.

Six blank spaces were drawn beneath the noose. The teacher then said the first word they were going to discuss in relation to slavery began with the letter "n" and ended with the letter "r."

Really. That's what he said.

The teacher then asked his fifth-grade students to guess the word.

Needless to say, the students started getting uncomfortable, especially the two Black girls. They looked around the class, and their White peers were looking right back at them. As the students remained silent, the teacher became adamant. He could not believe they couldn't figure out the word.

So, he wrote the word out on the board one letter at a time, n-i-g-g-e-r, and then he said it aloud.

That was how he started a lesson on slavery.

Of course, one of the Black girls went home traumatized. Fortunately, her mother was a civil rights attorney. Guess who got a serious letter and the threat of a lawsuit if they did not pull that curriculum and the social studies teacher? The principal did, and she initially stated she was unaware of the lesson and would need to investigate. It turned out it was not the first time that lesson had been taught by that particular teacher, and once the investigation was completed, the recommendation was made to have the lesson and teacher removed. From what we surmised, the matter was settled, and the parent was satisfied with the outcome, but there was very little discussion of how the school responded to the threat of the lawsuit, and the mother has remained silent about the incident to this day.

Another example is from one of our junior high schools within the same school district. There, a combination of all the seventh-grade classes went to a group assembly. There were approximately five Black students scattered throughout the auditorium. The other students were predominately White. The purpose of the assembly was to watch a movie on slavery. It was called Race to Freedom: The Underground Railroad. The 1994 film presents a very graphic depiction of slavery with brutal violence, lynching, and plenty of uses of the "n" word.

No disclaimers were given to the children before the movie was shown, and parents were never told their children were going to see it. Somehow, the educators at the school thought that movie would be a great and appropriate way to explain slavery to seventh-grade students.

Yet after the movie was shown, the Black children were heckled and ridiculed by their classmates. They were called the "n" word. They were told their ancestors were slaves; therefore, they were now slaves to the White students and needed to do what they were told.

It was appalling. One student even had to get an Individualized Educational Plan (IEP) so that she could have her phone with her at all times. Phones were not allowed in class, but she needed one so she could always get in touch with her mother because she was so fearful.

When Black Mothers Forum and the parents of the Black students talked to the principals of both schools, each one said they were not aware of the Hangman lesson or the movie. We were later given an educational sheet that indicated the district had approved the showing of the movie. That approval was based on information from the school administrators stating that they felt the only offensive words in the film were "Oh, God" and "hell."

Apparently, they did not believe the "n" word was offensive. The parents asked if teachers at either school had to turn in their lesson plans in advance. The principals told them it had been years since they had reviewed their lesson plans.

The involvement of Black Mothers Forum forced school district administrators to look at what was being taught and how. Arizona state academic standards stated schools were supposed to teach on the Civil War and slavery, but no specific directives had been provided on how and what that would look like. Our mothers wanted these subjects to be taught, but in a safe and appropriate way—with the right materials and the right people teaching them with the right intentions.

When first faced with such issues, we did not know how to advocate for our families. We also didn't know our rights. I approached Antonio at the civil rights organization we had been working with on this, and he told me about their training program called "Know Your Rights." We decided to have the mothers go through that training in October 2017. From there, we started getting involved in those disputes and advising parents what to do. More mothers started attending our meetings and sharing with other mothers what was going on in their schools. It was not uncommon to hear, "That's happening in my district, too? I thought I was alone."

They weren't—and the problems were far more prevalent than any of us would've believed.

The incidents at the elementary and junior high schools opened up a can of worms which uncovered decades of racial bullying in their school district. In January 2018, another incident occurred at the same junior high school after some eighth graders, White boys, had a gathering at a home the Friday before Martin Luther King Jr.'s birthday. A video was made where the kids were singing a rap song by Bobby 2 Pistolz, a White supremacist music artist, entitled "F*** All N***azs." The video was circulated through social media—and a beautiful mother of three lovely Black daughters, and a powerful protector mama whose daughter attended that school, showed it to me.

She told me that when she brought the video to the attention of the school principal, she quickly sent out an email saying that while the video was troubling, there was nothing more she could do. From what she had gathered, the White students had acquired the verbiage from a video from a Black rap group, Rah Digga (feat. *Young Zee* of Outsidaz). She said she was sorry the incident had happened, but that the White students involved would not be disciplined because the incident had occurred off campus and during non-school hours.

That simply wasn't going to work for us.

A prominent parent in the district looked up the words to the song, identified the artist, and went to the media on January 17, 2018. He also provided to the media the email from the principal, insisting she hadn't investigated anything but had cast it off as something a Black rap group had put out there, and these White children were merely repeating what they heard and sending it out via their social media networks. The parent asked the principal to apologize and to hold the children who made and distributed the video accountable for their actions.

The same parent reached out to Black Mothers Forum via email that same day, requesting to know how he could work with us to address this matter with the school and district. We partnered with several concerned Black families at the junior high school and started organizing meetings with these parents. A newspaper reporter was assigned to us, and the parents got a chance to tell the reporter their stories, how they felt about what had happened, and how the handling of the incident by the school principal and the district discounted the seriousness of racism within the district.

The principal came under so much pressure, she reached out to the school superintendent to ask what to do. I also talked to the superintendent, and I told her the principal had mishandled the situation. I told her that not only was the Black community upset in the east valley where the school district was located, but so were diverse groups of parents from across the state.

The superintendent was unmoved. She refused to reprimand the principal and claimed the incident did not violate school policies because it happened off campus.

Again, that simply wasn't going to work—so I looked up the code of conduct policy as it related to student violence, harassment, intimidation, and bullying. This policy is called JICK and is dated December 21, 2011. Under the definition for cyberbullying, it stated that "cyberbullying is, but not limited to, any act of bullying committed by use of electronic technology or electronic communication devices, including telephonic devices, social networking and other internet communications, on school computers, networks, forums and mailing lists, or other District-owned property, and by means of an individual's personal electronic media and equipment."

I told the principal and superintendent that the incident was cyberbullying because the video was taped on a personal device and had been circulated on campus and during school hours. The superintendent responded by saying she couldn't do anything without an official complaint being filed, so I took care of that, too. I found the school district's bullying form and had each of the Black parents of the impacted students complete the form and turn it in, hoping to force the district to launch a formal investigation.

Next, in adherence to district protocols, one of the mothers set up a meeting for the parents with the principal, and I planned to join them.

Sadly, the principal was so flustered, she called the superintendent's office again, insisting that she was afraid to have all of us show up at the school at the same time. The superintendent contacted me and asked that I not participate in the meeting. When I told her that parents wanted me to show up, she again asked me not to attend because it was making the principal nervous. I replied by telling her it was interesting to me that she would protect her principal when she was uncomfortable, but not protect the parents and children who were feeling the same way.

The superintendent promptly ended our call, and the next thing I knew, the assistant superintendent of secondary education, a Black male, contacted the mother who had initiated the meeting via email. He not only asked her to not have me attend the meeting, but to also have the other parents not attend, saying he'd be happy to meet with them, but that they didn't want everyone to show up to meet with the principal. He added that if everyone showed up at one time, he would have to call the police.

I told her to send the assistant superintendent an email and have him tell the police to meet us at the junior high school at 3:45 p.m. The meeting was scheduled to start at 4:00 p.m. Guess what happened? At 3:45 sharp, I was there with all of the other parents, the assistant superintendent of secondary education arrived, and there were no police.

Of course, there wouldn't be. It was just a parent's meeting with the school principal. No laws had been broken.

Administrators had tried to intimidate us, and it did not work.

We quietly went into the lobby of the school office, took our seats, and the nervous office staff proceeded to tell us the principal would soon see us. The principal came out into the school lobby with the assistant superintendent and stated that she had decided to meet with each parent individually, citing privacy issues. When a parent pointed out that they were all there to see the principal about the same thing, we were told it was the principal's individual policy to meet with one family at a time because she didn't know when something personal would come up.

She met with the first family for 45 minutes.

There were seven families. I told them all to start ordering pizza because we were going to be there the rest of the night.

After approximately two hours, when the principal realized the other families were not going to leave, she changed her mind, saying she'd go ahead and meet with everyone at once. We gathered in the school's conference room, and each parent shared their concerns about the incident and the circulation of the video and how it had impacted their children as well as the community. We got done by around 6:30 p.m. I served as a facilitator in the meeting, but the parents did much of the talking. The assistant superintendent remained silent as he took notes.

A couple of weeks later, the superintendent asked me to meet with her at her office to review everything that had happened. She said she had no problem engaging in this type of conversation, and that I brought up some good, valid points, but reiterated there was nothing they could do to discipline the students because they had done nothing wrong. The superintendent said the video was horrible, but the students didn't violate any policies by making the video or distributing it. I read through the policy on student violence, harassment, intimidation, and bullying, reviewed the policy on cyberbullying, and asked her for an explanation.

She couldn't provide one. The superintendent also commented that she hoped Black Mothers Forum could evolve to the point where one day it would no longer need to be called Black Mothers Forum, but just Mothers Forum. I told her that would not happen until our Black children started facing only the same types of circumstances and issues as White children.

I then gave the superintendent a challenge.

"This is a defining moment for you," I declared. "This will either show that you are a leader with courage, or it will show that you are no leader at all. Which one will it be?"

In the end, the district facilitated having the children who made and distributed the video, and their families, meet with a counselor for two hours to talk about racism. That was it. They did not have to apologize like requested. They were not reprimanded like requested. Any time our Black children did something someone thought was wrong, they were suspended. These children could offend an entire community, and they got counseling.

It was crazy.

Black Mothers Forum continued to press the issue with the school district, and the district even had a press conference saying they were not going to do anything else about the incident. That prompted the Black community to have its own press conference. Every community Black leader was there, from the various civil rights organizations to social justice-focused churches and ministers. White, Black, Hispanic, Indigenous people—every community showed up to cry out against what the school district was doing, and not doing, with these students and their families. We encouraged the Black parents and their children to speak at the school board meetings to share with governing board members the racial bullying they had encountered at the various schools within the district. We also exhorted them to share their disagreement with the district administrators' unwillingness to hold the offending eighth-grade students accountable for cyberbullying their Black classmates in accordance with their own school's antibullying policy.

Unfortunately, the district did not act on our concerns—and the situation escalated.

Threats were made against the families of the White eighth graders. Property damage occurred to their homes. People were leaving dog poop on their cars, breaking their car windows, and terrorizing their families through vandalism and verbal and written threats. Black Mothers Forum, along with other Black community leaders and parents, did not condone any of this activity—and we spoke out against it, telling the perpetrators to stop via media releases, press conferences, and statements at school board meetings.

Many community members exhibited anger and fear—and I made sure the superintendent was aware that it had all happened because she didn't step up and lead when she had the opportunity.

On February 14, 2018, over 100 White, Black, Hispanic, and Indigenous community members from all over Arizona showed up at the school district's governing board meeting. Many Black children from different schools in the district told their stories about the racial bullying they had endured with little to no acknowledgment by school administrators that any trauma had occurred.

The school board meeting started at 7:00 p.m. At about 8:30 p.m., in the middle of a Black parent expressing the pain that his daughter had been going through in her school as a result of the video, the board president stood up.

"I really, really care about this," she interrupted, "but I've got to go."

She left. It was Valentine's Day, after all.

The room erupted. Everybody spoke. The meeting didn't let out until close to midnight.

In the coming weeks, several meetings took place with various Black community leaders, governing board members, and district office staff. The governing board voted and approved an equity and inclusion resolution, committing funds to hire an equity and inclusion director. That person was hired in April 2018. She still served in that position three years later—but not without opposition. In March 2021, a Black teacher in the school district was scheduled to file a lawsuit against the district for discrimination against her. This teacher, who was on the original equity and inclusion team that the equity and inclusion director set up in 2018, told me that equity and inclusion teams had been established for each school that included training and conferences. Unfortunately, due to push back from White families and some White, male teachers, their efforts had been delayed. She claimed the White, male teachers did not know why they were being made to feel guilty about how they felt about a certain kind of people.

As a result, the superintendent's office had been urged to have the equity and inclusion director slow down and back up on some of the equity and inclusion team's efforts to give people time to absorb it and get comfortable with it. The teacher said a lot of the teams had since been disbanded. In addition, she said the equity and inclusion director had not been able to get involved in any disciplinary complaints as they related to Black students, effectively taking her out of the conversations.

The same thing has been happening with many of the equity and inclusion directors in other schools throughout the state of Arizona. Black Mothers Forum has allies on the inside who need a whole lot of support, and we continue to push from the outside in to make sure change happens to create safe and supportive environments for our Black children.

———

The last major event that Black Mothers Forum had to deal with prior to the writing of this book was in another school district that predominantly serves parts of Phoenix and its suburbs, Chandler, Tempe, and Guadalupe, along with portions of the Gila River Indian Community within our county. The district has a history of racially discriminatory practices, and in January 2018, we were contacted by a Black parent, Sharon, after she was referred to us by her NAACP chapter.

The incident involved her son, Herb, a seventh grader at one of the middle schools. He had been suspended for 10 days after returning to school from being on suspension for 10 days prior to that. According to Sharon, when her son was suspended the first time, he was accused of intimidating a White, female teacher. Herb had a math class across campus. His next class was science. The school's principal had announced that running on campus was no longer allowed.

That presented a problem for Herb. If he had to follow the rule and walk from math to science, he'd be late to science class. Instead of telling his mother he needed an accommodation made so he could get to class on time, he went to his science teacher, a White male teacher, and explained his situation. The science teacher told Herb it would be fine for him to walk and be late as long as the class wasn't disturbed by his tardy arrival. The science teacher also checked out Herb's story with the math teacher, and the math teacher admitted that she tended to keep her class late. The science teacher even walked the path Herb took and realized Herb was correct.

On January 31, 2018, the science teacher was out for the day, and his assistant teacher, a White woman, was left in charge of the class. When Herb arrived late from his math class, the assistant teacher stood outside the door and told Herb he couldn't come in. Herb reminded her that he had an agreement with the science teacher that he could be late as long as he didn't disturb the class when he arrived. She said the agreement was with him, not with her.

When she told Herb he needed to go get a referral, an excuse for being late, before he could come to class, Herb responded by saying that by the time he did that, he would have missed most of the class.

She said that was his problem, not hers.

Herb stomped his foot and told her that she was abusing her power. She directed him to go to the office, and then proceeded to call the office and report that Herb had threatened her. Ultimately, Herb was suspended for 10 days.

While Herb was at home, Sharon requested that her son be removed from the science class because the assistant teacher did not create a safe place for him. The principal said she would take care of it, but nothing was done. When Herb returned to school on February 15, the day after the horrific mass shooting in a high school in Parkland, Florida, he realized he was still in the same science class. Sharon said Herb went to the vice principal and was told the transfer would be taken care of, but that he had to go to class that day anyway and not say anything to the assistant teacher.

During lunch, Herb's friends asked him where he'd been while he was away from school. Embarrassed to tell them that he had been suspended, Herb was about to say that he'd been out ill. Before he could formulate his response, his friends told him that the assistant teacher from his science class had already told them that he'd been suspended. Herb was embarrassed and upset over the violation of his privacy rights as a student.

Sharon said Herb knew that what the assistant teacher had done was wrong, so he went straight back to the vice principal, insisting the teacher had "told his business" to his classmates. The vice principal told Herb that he didn't believe the assistant teacher would do that, and that Herb should still not say anything to her when he went to science class that afternoon. He was told to go to class and be quiet.

He did, but Herb said the assistant teacher was, as Sharon put it, "looking at him strange." Frustrated, Herb got upset and asked why she was looking at him. She said she wasn't, and he then asked her why she would tell his business to others. She said she didn't say anything, and he told her his friends had said she had told them. The science teacher then asked Herb to settle down and go take a break in the recovery room, a place on campus where students could go and calm down. Herb obeyed his science teacher and left—but after he departed the classroom, the assistant teacher called down to the office and claimed Herb had threatened to shoot her.

On his way to the recovery room, Herb was intercepted by school security and taken to the office. He was frightened as the vice principal searched his backpack and called Sharon to come and get him.

When Herb arrived at school the next morning, he was immediately sent to the vice principal, who stated that a White, female student had heard he was threatening to shoot someone at the school. Therefore, Herb was told to sign a paper that stated that he agreed to be suspended for another 10 days because he was deemed to be an imminent threat to the school and needed to be off campus immediately. Sharon was never contacted, and Herb, being a minor, signed the paper at the prompting of the vice principal without parental consent or legal counsel.

The following Tuesday, February 20, I joined one of our civil rights leaders in making an unscheduled visit to the middle school to meet with the school's principal. When the office receptionist asked if we were expected, we told her we weren't, but that we would wait. She told us the principal was in a meeting, and she wasn't sure when she'd be available.

Before our visit, I'd gone online to view a picture of the principal so that I'd be able to recognize her. Sure enough, as we waited, she came out, and I saw her walking around and casually talking to other people.

I walked up and tapped on the receptionist's window.

"It doesn't look like she is in a meeting to me. Can we meet with her now?"

Shortly thereafter, we were invited into the principal's office, and we told her why we were there. She said she didn't have permission to talk to us about a student without the parent's permission.

I'd anticipated that. I had Sharon and Herb outside, sitting in the car waiting for us.

I went to get them, and Sharon, Herb, Mr. Lewis, and myself followed the principal to her office. Her vice principal was waiting for us. We sat around a big rectangular conference table, with the principal sitting at one end and Mr. Lewis at the other. Herb sat next to the principal, and I sat between Herb and his mother. The vice principal was positioned directly across from Herb.

It was a pretty intimidating set up for Herb, and he started to shake uncontrollably. I tried to calm him down with a touch to his arm to reassure him he was not alone, but Herb continued to tremble throughout the meeting, and no wonder. The principal and vice principal proceeded to shift all of the blame onto Herb and did not once acknowledge any wrongdoing by the assistant teacher or themselves. When Mr. Lewis asked if school administrators had found any guns on Herb when his backpack was unlawfully searched without permission, he was told no guns were found. Mr. Lewis then asked, "Why was Herb sent home, and how was he considered an imminent danger, without any evidence of weapons to hurt or harm anyone?"

The response was silence—followed by an abrupt termination of the meeting, which had lasted approximately 45 minutes.

Three days after that meeting with the principal, Sharon received a letter from the school district's office stating that the principal had recommended that Herb be expelled—meaning that he would not be able to return to any school for the rest of the 2018-2019 school year.

A due process hearing was scheduled for February 28. Black Mothers Forum and nine other Black community leaders showed up to advocate for Herb and support him. District officials seemed surprised by the strong turnout. As a result of Sharon's tenacity and our involvement at the hearing, we were able to prove that Herb had no intention of shooting anyone and that he did not have access to any guns to do so. The hearing officer rescinded the recommendation to expel Herb, but still decided that Herb should be placed in an alternative school within the school district for the rest of that school year.

That meant Herb would have to be moved out of the gifted program, which devastated both Herb and Sharon. In the end, she moved her son to a different school district in the middle of the semester so that he could attend a gifted program. Because Sharon had other children in the school district, that created a hardship that took a heavy toll on her family.

Complaints were made by other Black families who attended the same school, such as an eighth-grade Black student who was called "a cotton picking 'n' word" during class by another student, a Hispanic male. When the Black student told his teacher what had happened, he was told to ignore it, take his seat, and get back to work. After being called the same thing for a third time, the Black, male student punched the other student in the face, and a fight ensued. The Black, male student was suspended for starting the fight, while the other student was not suspended because the teacher conveniently claimed that she didn't recall the Black student identifying exactly who was calling him the name.

> More parents began showing up at school board meetings to expose the racial bullying going on.

The Black, male student was subjected to a police interrogation by the local police department without parental knowledge or consent, or the presence of legal counsel. In fact, his mother didn't know anything had happened until school officials called to tell her to pick him up from school for a 10-day suspension.

More parents began showing up at school board meetings to expose the racial bullying going on at both the middle school and the school district's office and shared stories demonstrating the same lack of response to it. Subsequently, Black Mothers Forum conducted a press conference in front of the school district's office on October 23, 2018. It was held immediately following the governing board's disciplinary review study conducted during their executive session just prior to the general governing board meeting.

In the press conference, we pointed out the deficiencies in the study, and I addressed the district's request for more time to correct those deficiencies, saying that our children did not have more time and that we wanted the disproportionate treatment of our Black children to stop immediately. If the district requested more time to put equity and cultural competency measures in place, I added, then we expected our Black children to stop being disproportionately disciplined until their staff was properly trained to address the behavioral and safety needs of our children.

In February 2019, a video was released from an anonymous person at the middle school showing the principal making morning announcements to her students, stating that she did not believe in celebrating Black History Month or any culture's month. She said Black students should be responsible for putting together their own Black history celebrations, and that it was not her staff's responsibility to do so. That video was forwarded to me, and I subsequently released it through our Black Mothers Forum's social media since all of our previous attempts to have the principal removed had fallen on deaf ears.

After much media coverage over the principal's comments and past actions against Black students, the principal did leave her position in June 2019. She was replaced by another principal. The vice principal was also replaced with a Black, male vice principal. As of 2021, Black Mothers Forum has not received any more complaints from Black parents at that middle school.

It's clear. When we as Black mothers come together to be a voice and an advocate, there is power. That power has allowed us the opportunity to change oppressive systems within our schools to create more safe and supportive learning environments for our Black children. We are well on our way toward dismantling the school to prison pipeline and giving our sons and daughters a well-deserved chance to live up to their full potential and greatness.

In order for us as Black mothers to be fully ready and empowered to do this vital work—and to recognize the amazing giftings that exist within each one of us—we need to know and take ownership of the *characteristics* that form our anatomy as Black mothers. As we unfold these characteristics together, you will discover how each one is present in your life, and you will identify the characteristics that are strongest for you.

The anatomy of a Black mother—your anatomy—is made up of many incredible characteristics. We will focus on six of these:

- Warrior: Determined and Revolutionary
- Protector: Guardian and Shield
- Resourceful Resilience: Making Strategic Moves
- Determination: Immovable and Steadfast
- Leadership Courage: Truth to Power
- Wisdom: Wise Counselor

Anatomy of a Black Mother will define each characteristic, relate it to the unique challenges you face as a Black mother, and then personally introduce you to a Black mother who exemplifies that characteristic, presenting her story in her own words.

You will be educated, inspired, and infused to action as each one is presented to you.

We will begin with the Warrior.

Let's go to battle!

CHAPTER 1

WARRIOR:
Determined and Revolutionary

"Finally, be strong in the Lord and in his mighty power.
Put on the full armor of God, so that you can
take your stand against the devil's schemes."
~ Ephesians 6:10-11

When you look up the word "warrior" in a dictionary, you'll see a variety of definitions: "a person engaged or experienced in warfare," "someone involved in some struggle of conflict," or "a soldier or someone engaged in a fight." It is most frequently used to describe a person who is very strong and doesn't give up easily.

All of those definitions fit the description of a Black mother who is a warrior—but they only begin to scratch the surface as to the true extent of her tenacity and effectiveness when it comes to battling for her children.

Historically, Black mothers have had to defend the rights of their children and put in the necessary work to preserve their well-being in their schools and surrounding communities. We are determined to defend ourselves and our children, no matter what the cost. We exhibit our strength the most when faced with daunting and threatening situations, making us more determined to forge ahead with boldness and courage.

Inside each one of us resides resiliency and fortitude—a sense of inner strength that is manifest even when we cry. In truth, Black mothers weep a lot, but then we get back up with unrelenting perseverance. We have had to withstand the harsh realities of mindsets, policies, and systems designed to discourage our forward movement. Even in the midst of rejection and blatant disrespect for us and our children, we continue to push for equal and equitable treatment.

We as warrior mothers honor our opponents while, at the same time, not underestimating them. Black mothers who are warriors are very respectful, yet we will go to great lengths to show our opponents the error of their ways and how they can make the necessary adjustments in order to provide more equitable outcomes for our families. We take great pains to study, learn, and grow—and many of us have no problem with speaking our truths. We intentionally take our time to articulate what we want to see happen, and we expect to be a part of arriving at the solution. We no longer believe we need to wait on someone to give us permission to speak up for our rights. Our children need our advocacy now!

Above all, we as Black mothers give God all the honor, glory, and praise for each victory that we get to celebrate, as well as for our setbacks, because our setbacks set us up for our big comebacks. We believe our effectiveness as warrior mothers stems from the result of our prayers. As spiritual warriors, we see our painful circumstances as opportunities to draw us closer to the Lord.

As our warrior spirit comes forth, our focus only becomes clearer.

We grow more determined.

We grow more consistent.

We grow more revolutionary.

Of course, as we grow, we have to fight against stereotypes designed to paint us as emotionally irrational and out of control, which couldn't be further from the truth. For so long, any time a Black mother has raised an objection to anything as it relates to our children or our family members, we are portrayed as "angry Black women," hands on our hips, shaking our heads—and that may very well be true. We *are* going to take command of the situation when needed by pointing a finger in the face of anyone who has gone too far, and we will not be dissuaded from speaking our mind.

There is nothing wrong with that. We are passionate people. Yet it is exhausting at times to be constantly aware of how we are being perceived as Black mothers so that others, particularly White people, don't feel fearful of, or intimidated by, us.

We must manage all of this while being unrelenting in our pursuit to create a safe and supportive environment for our Black children with the attitude of, "I don't care how many times you put me out, I'm going to come right back. I don't care how many times you shut me down, I'm going to come right back." Our foremothers, who were enslaved, had to exhibit that same warrior-like perseverance. They had to have the courage to tell that small lie to the slave master so that their children would not be sold away from them because they looked physically strong or had some other capability perceived to be an asset to another slave owner which would forever separate them from their families. Oftentimes, Black mothers had to say their children were weak or sickly, playing down their strengths in order to keep their families intact and to protect their children from abuses both seen and unseen.

Unfortunately, this practice of diminishing the value of our children has passed down through the generations. I have witnessed Black mothers highlight the weaknesses of their children when others give them praise by saying things like, "Oh, they are not all that. Here's their shortcoming." More often than not, many of us have experienced the same kind of remarks from our own mothers. Unintentionally, we have doubted our true worth and even sabotaged our own greatness—and when our children hear us downplay their greatness, we, in essence, diminish their power and greatness. Unknowingly, we do this to take all eyes off of them, so they can safely navigate the oppressive educational and sociopolitical systems in place that are designed for their demise.

> As Black mothers, our concern for the safety of our Black children is real.

As Black mothers, our concern for the safety of our Black children is real, and we rightly wonder whether or not we will see our children come back through the front door alive. We also wonder whether or not our children will be seen as a threat or find themselves in a situation where they are exploited. Therefore, we have had to develop ways to cope and survive.

Conversely, many of the Black men in our community have had to downplay their manhood in order to survive, and they caution us to do the same. Yet we will no longer downplay our needs, our worth, or the racial injustices we encounter on a daily basis. "Oh, no," we'll counter. "We are going to speak to this. I know you don't feel like you can, but *we* will as Black mothers."

Felisha Taylor is a mighty warrior and a single mother of two Black sons who had to endure something I wouldn't wish on any other mother. Her oldest son, Nathaniel, was taken away from her when he was arrested at school and accused of heinous crimes that she knew he was not capable of committing.

This incredible Black mother displayed boldness, consistency, courage, fearlessness, strength, determination, prayer, and unrelenting perseverance in the midst of emotional, mental, and physical exhaustion as she relentlessly pursued the truth to secure the deliverance of her son.

It took just over three years, during which time Nathaniel was largely on house arrest, for Felisha to exonerate her son, and it was costly. Not only did Nathaniel lose experiences essential to growing up, like homecoming, prom, and graduation, but he was dehumanized to the point that he sometimes didn't want to go on living.

It was horrible—yet Felisha fought tenaciously for her child, and it was our honor at Black Mothers Forum to join her in this battle and see her and her family come out victoriously on the other side.

In the midst of our support of Felisha and her family, I personally witnessed Nathaniel come to terms with his humanity and his need for Jesus in his life. Nathaniel requested that I come to visit him to talk about what was going on inside of his heart. I was unaware of his inner struggle with God at the time. I met with Nathaniel and answered his questions about God, about Jesus, and about why the Lord would allow something like this to happen to him. After walking Nathaniel through the truths that he was created in the image of God, and that the Lord, at times, allows bad things to happen to good people, he recognized his need for Jesus to come into his heart and give him the peace he needed in the midst of his storm. That afternoon, I led Nathaniel in the sinner's prayer, and He accepted Christ into his heart.

I am convinced that if it hadn't been for the Lord entering his heart that day and giving him His peace that surpasses all comprehension, Nathaniel would not be celebrating the new season he is experiencing today in his life.

Here is Felisha's story, one of untold pain, unwavering trust, and unquestioned warrior power!

In Her Own Words

FELISHA TAYLOR
Written April 2021

I am a 39-year-old single mother of two boys. Nate turned 21 in March; my youngest, Marcus, turned 18 in December. I am also a foster mother to my baby niece, who was born last July with spina bifida, hydrocephalus, and Chiari malformation. I hope to be adopting her over the next few months.

I've been a mother for 21 years, all of that as a single mom, with the exception of a couple of years with Marcus' dad. I work hard to make sure that my kids are taken care of, and I love helping others, whether it is by giving someone a compliment or by making them feel good about themselves. Every day, I try to make sure that I am a better me than I was yesterday.

I also take mental health very seriously. You'll understand why as my story unfolds.

Nathaniel William Thomas was born in 2000—and the moment I looked at him I knew I was going to protect him, as his warrior, for the rest of his life. He started walking at nine months, so he has always been active. He was a happy baby, always getting into stuff. He loved to eat, and he still does. Food is life for him. Nate is funny, loves to make people laugh, and has an amazing smile. Nate has remained very close to me, I think, because it has always been just me and him. As a preteen, he became close to his cousins, and he is very protective over them—and me. He definitely didn't like guys trying to hit on me. He was not having that.

Nate always stood out at school. We lived in predominately White areas, so he was almost always the only Black kid in his classes. When Nate was in fifth grade, I began getting calls from the school about him tapping his pencil on the desk, bouncing his leg so his shoelaces knocked on the side of the desk, or being unable to stay in his seat. I met with the teacher, the principal, and the school counselor and psychologist, and they all told me to take Nate to the doctor because they thought he had ADHD. I took him in, along with paperwork we filled out at the school, and the doctor prescribed ADHD medication.

I don't want to say that it helped. It became more of an "I got in trouble today, but I forgot my medication," type of thing, and he just kept getting into trouble at school after that. It seemed I was always there, confused and arguing. "You are suspending my kid for three days because he was tapping his pencil on the desk? That doesn't make sense." I had to put him on an IEP, which I learned is an individualized education plan used for kids who need a little extra help but that don't have identified learning dis-abilities. I was told an IEP would be better for Nate because he would be placed into smaller classes.

From then on, I believe my son was being monitored too closely and just wasn't being allowed to be a kid. In sixth grade, for example, Nate and his classmates were doing arts and crafts using scissors. Nate was playing, and he chased one of the kids around the room. He wasn't doing or saying anything threatening, but because he had the scissors in his hands, the teacher said she felt he was a threat to the class, and he was suspended for 10 days.

Every single year it was something, and I wondered how my kid could be so different at school because at home he was such a good kid. Looking back, I feel like he was being paper trailed. Every school year he would go to a new teacher, and that teacher would already know what type of kid he was. I've since learned that it is standard practice for educators to make note of behavioral issues at school if they are problematic. Typically, those notes are placed online and are only available to each of the child's teachers as they progress, as well as the school counselor and principal. But this is done only in cases of a major, ongoing problem, and I can understand that for severe behavioral issues. But if there are only minor things, such as I felt was the case with Nate, why did it seem like he was being sent to the office every five minutes? That doesn't give children like Nate a fair chance because teachers have already set their minds on what the children are like, instead of allowing them to be who they are while determining whether or not they have deeper behavioral problems.

I didn't know what the school to prison pipeline was then, but I do now—and I am convinced my son was being placed in that pipeline.

As Nate progressed through middle school and into high school, he remained a super sweet kid. He cared deeply about other people's feelings, and he didn't like to see other people get hurt. He often came home from school and told me how he'd seen somebody bullying another classmate and felt he had to intervene.

Nate has always had a very sensitive heart toward others—which made what happened to him next that much more heartbreaking.

———

After living in Colorado for a while to help take care of my ill grandmother, my sons and I returned to Arizona in 2015. By then, I had decided that I wanted Nate to participate in a sport in high school in hopes that it might keep him out of trouble as well as give him an opportunity to earn an athletic scholarship for college. So, I specifically moved us close to one of the area high schools because they had a great football program. It had won several state titles since 2003.

Nate didn't really want to play football, but he played because he knew I wanted him to. He joined the junior varsity team as a sophomore and made the varsity team at the start of his junior year. As was usual for him, Nate made a lot of friends right away. A group of boys on the team came over to our house every weekend, and Nate sometimes went to their homes as well.

But as well as Nate was doing socially, the same couldn't be said in the classroom. It wasn't that he was doing poorly on his schoolwork, but he had one specific teacher who, in my opinion, didn't like him, so she made it tough for him. Before long, I requested that he be transferred out of her class, and we ended up having Nate attend one of the school district's learning academies part time. He took core courses there in the mornings, and then was bussed back to his high school in the afternoon so he could take Spanish, physical education, and of course, participate in football.

One Thursday afternoon in February 2017, I got a call from Nate. He was screaming and crying. He told me he'd just been kicked off the football team.

"What happened?" I asked.

"I don't know why I got kicked off the team. They hate me!" He didn't say much anything else because he was so distraught.

> "I don't know why I got kicked off the team. They hate me!"

I drove to the school, walked onto the field, and asked to see the head coach. He refused to talk to me. The assistant coach pulled me aside. "This is a bad idea," he said. "You shouldn't try to talk to him right now."

"Who else am I supposed to talk to? He is the one who kicked my kid off the team!"

I told the assistant that he needed to set up a time I could speak with the head coach. He scheduled it for the following Monday.

From Thursday to Sunday, I did my best to comfort Nate—and I did my research. I found a news story describing how the entire football team was sitting at a fast food restaurant across the street from their high school. They were being teenage boys: cussing, yelling, joking around, and the owner told them they had to leave. Some of them got disrespectful to the owner, and he had to call the police. The players were cited and were not allowed to go back onto the property.

I drove to the restaurant and requested to speak to the owner. He wasn't in, but he called me the next day. I introduced myself and explained who my son was.

"You know what?" the owner said. "I have a lot of issues with the coaching staff over there. Honestly, your son is the only person who walked back across the street, came back onto the property when he wasn't supposed to, and apologized on behalf of the football team." Then he added, "It wasn't even your son that was doing it. I am so sorry this happened."

Here's the kicker: the incident at the restaurant had happened six months *earlier*. So why was Nate, and only him, being kicked off the team now?

Monday, I met with the head coach, and Nate was there with us. I asked the coach for an explanation.

He leaned back in his chair. "He just goofs around too much, and he got in trouble at the restaurant. We can't have that type of person representing our team."

I couldn't believe he'd say something like that with Nate sitting right there. I pressed on, confronting the coach by revealing how I had spoken to the owner of the restaurant. "He told me that Nate was the one that went back across the street to apologize for the team."

The coach was dumbfounded. He didn't know what to say.

He put Nate back on the team.

Then, right before spring break in March, I got a call from the vice principal at my son's high school. He said Nate was being suspended for the rest of the week and that he could return to school after spring break. When I asked why Nate was being suspended, I was told it was because he had knocked a water bottle out of someone's backpack and that he had a video of the incident. He said it showed Nate and a friend stepping behind a girl and both simultaneously hitting the back of her bag with their hands, causing the water bottle to fall out.

I asked him if he would allow me to see the video. He refused.

"So, you are suspending my kid for knocking a water bottle out of a backpack?" The severity of the punishment didn't seem to match the crime. The timing of this seemingly unrelated incident with the earlier restaurant debacle also seemed sketchy to me. When I asked Nate about it later, he insisted that he and his friend were just playing, his friend didn't get punished, and he didn't understand why the school was doing this to him.

There was nothing more I could do. Nate was suspended.

My confusion, frustration, and sense of powerlessness grew. I knew my child better than they did, better than anyone. But I couldn't get anywhere.

When Nate returned to school on March 29, 2017, he had come from his father's house. I had been working an overnight shift at my job, so I was asleep when I got a call from the school's automated system around 9:00 a.m. It said Nate had been absent from his first two classes at the learning academy.

I immediately called Nate. He was still at his father's house, and he told me he didn't feel good and didn't want to go to school. Nate genuinely sounded like he wasn't feeling well, but I still told him that he needed to get up and get to school, or else I was going to go over and take him there myself. He promised he would, we hung up, and I went back to sleep.

Next thing I knew, the phone was ringing again. I looked at the clock by my bed. It was after 11 o'clock.

The call was from a female detective at our local police department.

She said Nate had been arrested.

I was befuddled. *Surely, they have the wrong person.* I thought.

"Arrested for what?" I asked.

She listed the charges. Sexual assault. Child molestation. There were nine in all.

I was incredulous. "No!" I insisted. "You have the wrong kid. This doesn't make sense."

The police had taken him into custody sometime after he arrived at school that morning. She told me where Nate was, and I asked if I could go there. By then, I was out of bed and getting ready.

"No," she said. "It doesn't make sense to come right now because you are not going to be able to talk to him."

"Absolutely not. You can't talk to him without me," I responded. "He is a minor. You don't have permission to talk to my son. I'll be right there."

I cut off the call, and all I can remember doing next is screaming at the top of my lungs.

I didn't understand what was happening.

When I got to the police department, the detective greeted me and escorted me into a room. She did not look the least bit friendly, but I couldn't worry about that. I had only one thing on my mind.

"Where's my son?" I demanded. "I need to talk to my son right now!"

The detective seemed irritated, and she definitely had an attitude. "Are you aware of the charges against him?"

"You told me already. I want to talk to my son."

The detective blurted, "You're not talking to your son."

I was so blown away by how rude and antagonistic she was. I could only imagine how they were treating Nate. "I don't have permission to talk to my son," I again declared. "Where is he?"

"He might be facing adult charges, so we are treating him as an adult." She then reiterated that I could not see Nate or talk to him. "Is there anything you want to tell me?" she asked accusingly.

I slammed my hand down on the table between us. "About what? I just want to see him. I want to talk to him right now!" I was so upset. I just sat there and stared at her, trying to process what was happening.

When the detective was done, she walked me back out to the front lobby. "I'll let you know if he will be released or not within the next hour." With that, she left.

All I could think about was what Nate was going through at that moment. It was unreal.

There were a few other mothers there—moms of other students who apparently had been arrested at the same time Nate had been. They were just as confused as I was. Some of Nate's friends began texting me. "It's a lie," they typed. "Don't believe them, Miss Felisha." Friends started calling me. "It's going to be okay," they encouraged. "Don't stress." When one of the moms got to go to the back, I thought maybe I would get to see my son after all. My mind wouldn't stop. *This is just a big mix up. This can't be.*

About a couple of hours later, the detective returned carrying a Ziploc bag containing a bracelet my son had worn that morning and some paperwork. She informed me that Nate was being processed and sent to a facility in nearby Mesa, Arizona, where I could either contact them or Nate would contact me later.

I was told to leave.

That was it. My son, suddenly an accused criminal, was going to jail—and I couldn't say or do anything about it.

———

I went to my godmother's house, sick to my stomach with stress. Shortly afterward, my aunt texted me, asking if Nate had been arrested. She said she'd seen it on the news. Heart pounding, I turned on the TV. Multiple channels were blasting stories about the incident. At that point, Nate hadn't been named or shown.

A few hours later, my son called me.

"Hey, mom. Are you coming to get me?"

"No, Nate. They are taking you to be booked in."

"What?" he said. "I didn't do anything. I didn't do anything, mom!" He was panicked.

"Nate, don't talk to nobody. Don't say anything to anybody. I don't care who it is, what they tell you, or who they tell you they are. You do not talk to anybody on the phone or in person unless it is me. Do you understand me?"

He started crying. "I love you," I told him gently, "and I'm gonna get you out of there."

I knew I needed to get an attorney, but I had no idea what kind of lawyer to get or what I was supposed to do. I'd never had to use an attorney before. I went with someone who was referred by a friend, and we met at a restaurant down the street from the Mesa courthouse the next morning.

Right after the attorney began discussing the situation with me, he got a call.

"I'm so sorry," he said. "They are not releasing Nate. They are sending him downtown to charge him as an adult."

Again, I didn't understand what was happening. "What do you mean? He is not an adult. He's a kid."

The attorney then told me to go home, saying he would call if anything changed.

I felt like I'd been dismissed—and, again, was utterly powerless.

That night, when I returned home, the TV news reports showed Nate's name and face for the first time. The caption below his picture identified him as a child molester charged with sexual assault.

I ran into the bathroom screaming. I started banging the cabinets.

He was a *child*—my child! To this day, I don't even know how to explain how I felt at that moment.

Over the seven days Nate was in custody, he called me every single day at 7:00 a.m. and 7:00 p.m., but we couldn't talk about anything having to do with the arrest or his charges. It was just, "How are you doing?" "Are you okay?" That week was pretty much a blur for me. I had to be sedated a few times so I could sleep. I was a complete wreck.

On April 5, over 200 kids, adults, parents, and grandmothers showed up for his evidentiary hearing. They filled the entire courtroom and overflowed into the hallways. Everyone told me how much they loved my son, and how they didn't believe what was being said about him. They said he was an amazing kid. When the judge announced Nate's bond at $25,000, the father of one of the football players walked right up to me and said he was going to take care of it. He then walked down the street to the bank and returned with the entire bond in cash.

> It was at that moment that I knew this whole thing was bigger than Nate.

It was at that moment, after everything that had happened the previous week and witnessing the incredible love and support for my son, that I knew this whole thing was bigger than Nate.

The next day, Nate was released when his bond was posted. We had our first in-person conversation when we got home. I asked him to tell me what had happened at the school.

"Mom, we were all just playing around, and we didn't even do what they are saying we did."

"Nate, I need you to tell me. I need you to trust that you can tell me anything. I don't care what it is. I have to know how to fight for you."

"Yeah, we slapped people on the butt. Yeah, okay, we did that, but mom, they are saying I stuck broomsticks up people's butts. I didn't do that. I didn't stick my fingers in people's butts. I didn't. I didn't!"

I felt like when I questioned Nate it made him feel like I didn't believe what he was saying and pushed him away. "I know this is hard, and I know that the police were in your face asking you, but I need to know."

He was insistent. "Mom, I'm not lying to you. I'm telling you the truth."

I believed my son.

I wasn't even allowed to enter the courtroom for Nate's arraignment on April 13. I had to watch it with the other parents outside the room on a TV. It broke my heart to see Nate sitting there by himself. He was shivering. Afterward, he said he was cold and wanted to come home.

There was more to the story. Nate was a little pawn in something else much larger than even the charges against him.

During the first week he was home, one of the other mothers, whose son had been arrested and was still in juvie, told me that someone had contacted her and wanted to help us. I was skeptical because I didn't know who I could trust. She asked if she could bring that person over to meet with us, and I reluctantly said she could.

Nate answered the door, and the moment I saw Janelle Wood, I knew she was supposed to be there. As she started talking to me, I saw that her concern was genuine. She really did want to help me. When Janelle asked if she could pray with us, she wanted to know if there was anything I wanted to pray about. I told her to pray for my son's mental health. She grabbed my hand and started praying.

After that interaction, I knew Janelle was going to be a part of our story. I knew I could trust her and share with her what little information I had.

One of those bits of information was the police report. I received it four days after Nate's release, and as I tried to read it, I couldn't understand how or why Nate had even been arrested in the first place, much less why he was moved to adult court. The report listed multiple people, pretty much everyone on the football team. There had to be up to 50 children listed in the report. Over 200 people were interviewed.

Why was my son being singled out? Why was it written and geared toward Nate?

I read that police report over and over again. I stayed up one time for three days straight. I bought little sticky notes. I had notecards and poster boards. I covered an entire room with it all, like you'd see a detective do on television.

But I couldn't make any sense out of anything the police report said. One item I couldn't get past was the fact that the kid who made the first accusations admitted that he had exaggerated his story. *What does that mean?* I wondered. *Can his story even be believed?*

I trusted Nate's attorney to do the right thing for us, but he was no help at all. Not only did he fail to give me any information, but he even had the audacity to say it was lucky I was "cute" because that was the only reason that he allowed me to be a part of the attorney-client conversations and shared with me what was going on. I guess since Nate was being considered an adult, nobody was legally required to tell me anything, including his attorney. But for him to actually say that? It was insulting.

In the first seven months from the time Nate was charged, that attorney was handling our case. Nate had to go to court every month—and every month, we'd be given another court date. Nothing was happening. Even worse, though, was that the attorney had Nate take a lie detector test and undergo a psychosexual evaluation—the latter, he said, to show that the boy's locker room play was not intended to be sexual in nature. When I took Nate in for the evaluation, I was told it was going to take up to five hours. The attorney hadn't said anything about that. I had no idea it was going to take that long.

Three hours later, I was contacted to come pick up my son. When I arrived, I found Nate sitting in the waiting room. He was fuming.

"What is wrong?" I asked as he got up so we could leave.

"I'll tell you in the car," he replied as he scooted past me. He couldn't wait to get out of that office.

When we got inside the car, my son busted out in tears.

"Mom, do you know what they just did to me? They made me look at all these nasty pictures."

"What are you talking about?"

He then said they showed him pictures of little kids and babies and asked questions like, "Do you get erect looking at things like this?"

I was shocked. Nate had just turned 17. I began crying because he was so upset—and I felt horrible. I had no idea what I had agreed to have done to my son.

We went to my sister's house to surround Nate with family. She has four boys who all love Nate. When we walked in the door, they ran to him, just like they had always done before. But Nate stopped dead in his tracks and backed up. That's how traumatized he was.

Later, when we got home, Nate went to his bedroom—and he stayed there for the next three days. During that time, he opened up to me when he could. He told me how what he saw at the evaluation made his mind think about things he would have never thought about otherwise. He said he was now uncomfortable playing with other kids because of what he had been asked and seen. I tried to encourage him. "If you didn't feel that way, something would be wrong. It is okay to feel that way."

More than once, I told my son how sorry I was that he had to go through the trauma of being introduced to anything having to do with pedophilia. "I'm upset that people think I'm a child molester," he'd respond.

That was what really hurt him the most. Nate was so good with kids. He loved being with children.

After that, I began losing trust in that attorney. Then I discovered that he had been sending in motions, on Nate's behalf, and without my knowledge or input, saying that Nate was guilty, but didn't mean to do anything.

Not once did the attorney ask Nate for his side of the story.

That was it. I called a family meeting, we decided to fire the attorney, and we hired a new one, a female. Within two weeks, almost a year into the case, she was able to provide me the entire police report and the video from the interviews.

It was the first time I was actually able to see something of substance—and what I saw was a witch hunt. The way the detectives were questioning the kids and the stories the kids were giving? I felt like everything was being done to implicate Nate.

It was around this time that a lawsuit was filed against the district and several administrators by five unnamed students. It came after a police investigation uncovered a web of secrecy to cover up the hazing incidents. All this time, Nate was under house arrest with an ankle bracelet. He was only allowed to go to school, work, and to the gym. He had to be in the house by 8:00 p.m.

He wasn't allowed to leave the house before 6:00 a.m. He had no internet or social media access of any kind.

My kid, who had always been happy, joyful, and full of life, became a recluse. They took away everything. Nate was expelled from the school district. I had to enroll him in a school Janelle found for him, but he had to take the city bus there every day. They took away all his friends, too. They had investigated and interviewed so many people that nobody who was involved in the case was allowed to even talk to him.

Nate was not doing well. He was depressed. I took him to a therapist and a psychiatrist. He was prescribed medication with side effects that negatively affected him physically and mentally. In one instance, Nate took medication to try to overdose. He was in and out of mental health facilities because he was cutting his arms.

I thought my son was going to kill himself.

It was horrible.

I met regularly with the second attorney, and she had her people going through everything to try and find the smoking gun. She was very thorough and found inconsistencies—such as the fact that some of the alleged sexual assault happened at a football camp that Nate didn't even attend, and that the abuse was happening with freshman players that Nate wasn't even around. One of the students alleging the assault was the son of a former National Football League player whose name was immediately removed from all discussions of the matter.

Despite all that, the attorney ultimately said there wasn't anything she could do. She said Nate was going to have to take a plea.

I refused—as did Janelle. "No, this doesn't make sense," she said to the attorney. "We are not going to allow you to throw him under the bus. We need someone who is going to fight for us."

"That is just how it is," the attorney countered. "Innocent people have to take pleas."

With that, I lost all trust in her, too. From that point on, I became suspicious of everything that attorney did. It got to the point where I had to decide that the lawyers actually worked for *me.* Nobody cared that my son was trying to kill himself because he was completely secluded from the life he knew. So, I had to become like a lion. I was a beast.

No one was going to take advantage of Nate or myself.

No one was taking down my son.

Nate was my first born. He knew I was the only person he could honestly, deeply trust. So, the only way I could keep Nate from feeling like the world was crumbling and falling on him was to be positive. Whenever we came out of yet another court appearance, we would have a normal conversation. We wouldn't talk about the case.

Everything in my life became about protecting my son— no matter the cost, even if it meant sacrificing my own mental health. Once, I literally slept for four days straight. I had to do it at the mental health facility. They knew who I was because my son had been there, so they allowed me to be there. My whole world became absorbed with Nate and the case against him. We continued to interview attorneys until we found one who we felt genuinely believed my son was innocent and would fight for Nate's freedom and future.

After three years, with Felisha's reluctant acceptance, Nate took a plea agreement and pled guilty to misdemeanor charges, not including any sexual assault charges, with six months of probation. That was on February 28, 2020. Nate had to wear an ankle monitor that entire time.

While he does not have any felonies on his criminal record, Nate still continues to experience roadblocks to furthering his education and securing gainful employment because he was involved in such a high-profile case. Together with prayers, Felisha, our Black mothers, and the right attorney, we were able to save Nate from going to prison, but there are still barriers being placed around him to limit his upward movement, such as background checks, financial aid restrictions, and the stigma of what he was accused of doing. It didn't matter that we were successful in proving his innocence in court. The media had painted Nate as a monster, and Felisha continues to do everything she can to make sure her son is seen as the caring and loving individual he is.

As a warrior mother, Felisha never gave up on her son. She never believed the negative reports about him. She never accepted the status quo when it came to cases like the one faced by her son, and she continued to challenge her attorneys to do their job and give Nate his life back. Today, he is living his young adult life and does not take it for granted. Instead, he is choosing to experience his best life and be the man he was created to be—a masterpiece!

CHAPTER 2

PROTECTOR:
Guardian and Shield

"No weapon forged against you will prevail, and you will refute every tongue that accuses you."
~ Isaiah 54:17

A protector is defined as someone who covers others from exposure, injury, damage, or destruction. As Black mothers, our entire role as protectors is to keep our children safe from all hurt, harm, or danger. We are here to preserve and guarantee that their needs are met free from exposure to any attacks or destructive measures that are placed in their way to derail their ultimate purpose.

In my work, I have watched Black mothers come together as protectors of the rights of our children to grow and learn in safe spaces. We also see ourselves as the guardians of our children's overall well-being, and we act as shields when our children are faced with overwhelming circumstances that they haven't the skill set to address. We set up guardrails to protect our children's emotional, mental, and physical well-being—and we possess an innate sense of when they are in danger and quickly erect those invisible and invincible shields around our children to divert potential emotional, mental, physical, or verbal abuse or harm.

It is natural for us to challenge individuals who foster behaviors, policies, and practices that create fear and instability in our children. When our children's behaviors are perceived as a threat, and they face punitive penalties as a result of these misperceptions, we step into position to create a barrier between those in authority and our children. This reveals our true guardian nature. The true protector mother goes into motion and all shields are activated.

Historically, Black mothers have been the ones who stood in front of false accusations and misconceptions about our Black children and set the record straight. Within the Black family and in our community, we work to preserve the very existence of our people. Without Black mothers standing in the position of protector, many of the Black men and women who have been responsible for fighting for our civil rights would not have had the undergirding they needed, or perhaps would not have even existed in the first place.

How do these mechanisms of protection work? First, we naturally move our children behind us and begin to verbally articulate how we feel about what is happening to them. This includes the trauma experienced due to being misunderstood, and the need to respectfully engage our children moving forward. Secondly, we begin to remind those in authority, now seen as offenders, about what we expect as they engage our children, and we ask questions about the credentials of the offenders and about what they are planning to do to resolve our children's trauma and create the safe and supportive environments they deserve. Thirdly, we want the offenders to apologize to our children for the trauma they caused, and we demand that every measure must be taken to ensure that they are not traumatized again.

When a Black mother has to show up to any space—be it at school, the police department, a city council meeting, or a town hall meeting—it means that she had to give up something, whether it was to leave her place of employment or step away from caring for a family member to do so. Her essential routine is disrupted, and when that happens, there will be some sort of agitation and aggravation, especially when she does not see her child as a threat to anyone.

It makes her ask, "Why do my child's behaviors and mannerisms tend to be criminalized and not normalized?" "Why are certain mannerisms that are not seen as a threat by me seen as a threat to the broader community?" "Why are we, as Black mothers, automatically expected to be patient and understanding when our children are singled out in school or when our unarmed Black children are murdered by police officers who took an oath to protect and serve their community, which includes our children?" "Why are we expected to own someone else's discomfort without them taking any responsibility for our discomfort?"

The determination and strength exhibited by my friend, Janice Varnado, further supports the protective power of a Black mother. As a guardian for our Black children, this shield of protection gives our children the courage they need to stand up for their right to be treated with dignity, fairness, and respect. A shield symbolizes defense and covering, and as Black mothers, we have extensive practice in shielding our children from people with hateful hearts and oppressive systems. Our work as a

> As Black mothers, we have extensive practice in shielding our children from people with hateful hearts and oppressive systems.

protective guardian shield for all of our children remains intact no matter how old they are or where they live.

We are a force to be reckoned with. Any questions?

JANICE VARNADO
Written September 2021

I have always been a protector. It started when I was a little girl growing up in Chicago, Illinois. In part, I was inspired by two very different superhero characters who had one very important thing in common.

Underdog was a cartoon series that was on television into the early 1970s. Whenever villains appeared, Shoeshine Boy transformed into Underdog, almost always to protect Sweet Polly Purebred from the bad guys. His saying was, "When help is needed, I am not slow, It's hip-hip-hip and away I go! There's no need to fear—Underdog is here!" I loved him because, as an underdog himself, he needed to be represented, but I felt I was like Underdog because I tried to take up for people who were being mistreated.

In contrast to that canine hero, Wonder Woman, first appearing in DC Comics in 1941, was originally sculpted from clay by her mother Queen Hippolyta and was given life as an Amazon warrior, along with superhuman powers as gifts by the Greek gods. Her television and film characterizations have had different adaptations, but she remained the same warrior woman who fought diabolical foes male or female, large or small. She wielded Bracelets of Submission and hurled the Lasso of Truth, with which she executed justice. I've always admired strong women who could get the job done.

But the reason both Underdog and Wonder Woman resonated with me was because they came against bullies. I hate bullies—and I have always wanted people who are bullied to know that they *matter*.

It wasn't until later in my life that I realized I do that because I wanted to know *I* mattered as a youngster as a result of what happened between me and my father. I felt like he was a bully because he was a very critical person, always overanalyzed, and had a lot of expectations of others. My parents had me when they were in high school and never got married. My father ended up moving away to California when I was two, so I didn't grow up with my dad, but was raised by my mom and my grandparents. My mom showed her strength as a protector by being a provider. My grandfather played more of the father role in my life. He wasn't a man of many words, he worked hard, and he took care of the family. He protected me and had no tolerance for bad behavior from adults. He was stern, and he would say what was on his mind without being critical. My grandmother was also a protector who made sure my emotional needs were met. She never saw bad in anybody and never talked badly about anyone, but if she didn't like someone's behavior, she stayed away from them.

I loved my grandparents, and I still feel grandparents should play a very important role in a child's development. It wasn't until I was eight years of age that my father's mother and I started visiting my dad together for a few weeks every summer.

Back then, I really didn't like my father very much. I resented the way he behaved. I thought it was completely the opposite of how a father should act. Yet now, as an older adult who has heard many horrible stories from others about their experiences with their parents due to abuse, I realize I don't really have anything to complain about. No, I didn't feel the way most girls do with their fathers, like a daddy's girl. I might not have liked my father's personality. But there was no harm done to me physically. In fact, years later, after I had moved from Illinois to Arizona, I was able to see my father, and I got years of stuff off my chest with him. I didn't tell him everything, but I told him enough that it gave him something to think about. He didn't realize how I felt, and it hurt him—but that changed our relationship. I recognize today that he could only do the best with who he was because he had wounds from his past. But as a child, you feel that your dad, your parents, should be your protectors.

A big reason why I am part of Black Mothers Forum is because I believe our kids need to be protected.

———

As a youngster, then, being a protector came intuitively to me. Since I grew up as an only child, it was through other families that I could serve my Underdog or Wonder Woman roles. The Jones family, for example, had no less than 16 people, so their relationships were interesting to me. *Wow!* I thought. *How can anybody have this many kids?* It was amazing to me. One of the people I felt the need to protect was Blue Eyed Jack. Her name was actually Dorothy, but the pirate-sounding nickname came from a birthmark in which the white part of one of her eyes was blue. Whenever the Jones family got into arguments, they always talked about Dorothy's eye. That hurt her feelings. One of Dorothy's siblings, Annette, had a disease where a large portion of her scalp was scaly. It was bald and almost looked like elephant skin, and she got teased about that.

One thing about the Jones family, though. They might have talked about each other, but when it came to someone else trying to mess with them, it didn't happen. When anyone else came against them, they banded together and closed ranks. Still, that didn't keep me from wanting to protect Dorothy and Annette from the bullies in their own home.

It was natural, then, that my older cousin, Iristine, from my mom's side of the family, caught my attention. All of their personalities were docile, the very opposite of how I felt my dad was—but Iristine was the type that everyone knew not to bother. She didn't play. Nobody was going to mess with her. Nobody bullied her. She dated one guy who used to drink a lot, and I guess he thought he was going to be able to physically abuse her, but she wouldn't have it. Years later, she had to do the same thing all over again with a different man. Iristine really was like Wonder Woman to me.

When I got to grade school, it seemed like there was always somebody in one of my classes each year that others would make fun of. Debra M. was fat and tall. She looked almost like an adult, and she got teased because she was such a big girl. Meanwhile, Debra K. wasn't as tall, but she was very overweight. She had dirty fingernails, her hair was not clean, and the other students made fun of her because they felt like she didn't take a bath. She was always sad. Few people talked to her. I believe she was being abused at home, and I felt sorry for her.

This compulsion, this *need*, to stick up against bullies to protect others makes sense. After all, I wasn't really able to take up for myself with my father when we were around other people because I needed to respect my elders. It was wrong to talk back to your parents in a certain manner. Since I felt bullied by him because I couldn't protect myself, anybody else who reminded me of him would set me off. I would've loved to have had my own protector as a child, but I didn't really have one. So, I wanted to protect others because I was acting out what I would've liked to have seen happen in my own life.

Like any other protector, though, I needed to be mindful of my actions. I became fixated with knives at an early age. My grandfather had a pretty, pearl-handled pocketknife. The handle was probably a little longer than a nail clipper, and when it opened up, the blade was about the same size. It was a tiny thing, but I really, really liked that knife. I didn't want to stab anybody with it, but I did (kind of) when I was 10 years old. It happened when the police chief's grandson, who was a year or so younger than me, tried to reach up my skirt while I was climbing a tree in the backyard. I had shorts on underneath, but it was still inappropriate. When he touched me, I jumped down, fell on top of him, and began beating him in the head. I remembered the knife was in my pocket, so I took it out, flipped the blade, and jabbed him in the arm.

I don't remember if there was blood, and he wasn't seriously hurt, yet I got punished anyway. The knife was taken away from me, and I couldn't go outside for a week. But the boy knew I meant business.

I think Iristine would have been proud of me.

Finally, an important part of my identity as a protector came from the fact that Emmett Till's mother, Mamie Mobley, was my fifth grade teacher. Emmett's story is well-known. Born and raised in Chicago, Illinois, he was visiting relatives in rural Mississippi in August 1955 when he spoke to 21-year-old Carolyn Bryant, the White, married proprietor of a small grocery store. He was accused of flirting with or whistling at Bryant, though what actually happened was never fully determined. Nevertheless, Till's incident with the woman apparently violated the unwritten code of behavior for a Black male interacting with a

White female in the Jim Crow-era South. Several days later, Bryant's husband and half-brother went to Till's great-uncle's house and abducted Emmett. They took him away, beat, and mutilated Emmett before shooting him in the head and sinking his body in the Tallahatchie River.

All those years later in her classroom at school, we could see how the horrific event affected Ms. Mobley because she was a very intense, serious person. She didn't smile. She seemed miserable.

Just thinking about what she must've gone through as a parent made me want to protect others all the more.

As a protector of others, and even myself, I did what I had to do—a tenacity that only grew as I became an adult. I have two kids, a daughter and a son. My daughter is the oldest, and from her I have two grandchildren, twin girls. I knew I was in for the battle of my life as a mother after my daughter, a nurse, went through a long, terrible divorce battle that ended up lasting for years as they went back and forth in court. I don't want to see anyone go through what she has gone through in the justice system. I remained with my daughter every step of the way. Whenever she had to go to court, it was quite an overwhelming process for her. Sometimes it seemed the justice system does everything it can to victimize the person who is the victim.

Such is the life for the protector mama. It brought out the protector in me for her and my grandkids. Nothing or no one is going to stand in my way. I consider myself a Mama Bear, and I will protect my cubs.

When I was 34 years of age, I left work as an administrative assistant in corporate America, some of it doing temp work, to take a position in Palatine, Illinois with the United States Postal Service in 1991. I figured I could make more money working at the post office, but after I started, I hated it because of the hours and the labor. It felt almost as if I was doing factory work.

I certainly didn't seek to be union steward there, but there were so many different issues going on in the workplace. It was like we didn't have any rights at all, and I went directly into protector mode for my fellow workers. A few people referred to me as Rosie the Riveter, the character featured on posters during World War II that represented women who worked in American factories and shipyards during the war. I had that type of personality.

During my tenure as union steward, I'll always recall the day I was asking people to participate in an upcoming donation drive for the Red Cross and the Salvation Army. I approached a fellow employee that I hardly knew, but every time I got close to her, she'd shy away from me, almost as if she were afraid. Determined, I tried to speak to her as I walked toward her, but we were near a loud mailing machine, and she must've thought I was yelling at her. She went to the manager, and I was called into the office and accused of harassing her.

I was shocked until the manager shared that the employee had a hard time trusting people because of a few bad life experiences. He didn't go into any details, but he said she was very upset and that I shouldn't talk to her. As time went on, I did get to know her, and as I did, I gained a better understanding of her story. We became friends, and I became her protector from then on.

I worked at the post office for about seven years before moving to Chandler, Arizona. I had come out west to visit a friend and a relative, and I fell in love with the weather, the desert environment, and the far lower cost of living compared to Chicago. My main reason for moving to Arizona, though, was to protect my son, who was in sixth grade at the time, from the streets and gang life of Chicago. He was at the prime age when gangs started to recruit young boys. One incident had already occurred, and I removed him from that particular school. We came here to visit shortly after that incident, and we returned to stay two months later. I haven't looked back since.

I first trained to be a loan officer before working as a relay operator for the deaf- and hearing-impaired community. Eventually, I got a position with a major insurance company before being employed by the State of Arizona Department of Insurance as an advocate on behalf of consumers with different insurance-related complaints.

I also became a protector for people who were being denied insurance. In one case, I advocated for a man who had throat cancer and had lost half of his tongue as a result of the radiation treatments. He was in advertising, so using his voice was an essential part of his profession. He sought long-term disability, but the insurance company denied his request after making several calls to his home and determining that he didn't need the benefits. That really disturbed me, and I fought for him. Unfortunately, I was not successful.

Another situation involved a professional football player who, because of his job, needed to use an insurance market to seek a million dollar policy. The insurance company battled against the market, and it went to court to try to stop me from obtaining his records as his advocate. The state governor was even contacted. They really wanted me to leave the case alone. But I refused, and ultimately, I helped him win, in large part due to my tenacity and the support of my direct manager. I later received a letter from both the client and his attorney, thanking me for not letting it go.

I went back to school and got my bachelor's degree in human services management in 2010 and my master's degree in education in 2014. In 2013, I became a commissioner on the Human Relations Commission for the City of Phoenix, where I served to make sure that all city employees, companies, and organizations were working to eliminate discriminatory practices. Today, I am an academic counselor for the University of Phoenix, where my main task is to partner with students to help them successfully complete their programs from start to finish and beyond to achieve their career goals. If they happen to go into academic probation because of their grades, I help them stay on track and create strategies to get past the issues they are going through so they can successfully complete their program.

In many ways, an academic counselor is equivalent to being a psychologist or therapist. I hear the students' problems, and some situations have left me in tears. One of my students was struggling in class. She had missed several assignments, and I just knew something was wrong. It turned out she had a four-year-old daughter who had been molested by her female preschool teacher. The student told me she had been in a pretty bad place, and as she took me through the whole scenario, it simply broke my heart. While she was talking to me, my tears started. I let her get through everything she needed to say, but I was so choked up, she ended up comforting me. I stayed on the phone, but I could not speak. It was the first time that I was ever totally speechless. I've also had students who were going through the death of family members, suicide, or domestic violence. I called one student to check in on her because of an issue with her grades, only to discover she was in the hospital because she had been victimized by domestic violence. It was so sad; she could barely talk or see. My students often tell me that they originally had no intention of sharing so much with me, but I have a comforting voice, and I protect them by providing a safe place where they can talk.

I have also served as a mentor with the Fresh Start Women's Foundation. Its original mission was to help military wives who may have been through a divorce and didn't have the skills to get back into the workforce. It eventually broadened its services to all women, and I was one of its mentees. I credit Fresh Start's influence with helping me go back to school to get my degrees. As a mentor, I dealt with other women who want to go back to school or who have experienced domestic violence. It was my hope to motivate and empower them to be all they can be.

I found out about Black Mothers Forum in 2016 through Gwen Payton, my church's Sunday school teacher. I was drawn to Gwen because her spirit reminded me so much of my grandmother. She shared with me how Black Mothers Forum was getting ready to do advocacy-related work, and I was interested in learning more, especially as I thought about the times I had to protect my children from bullying and inequality in the educational system.

Of course, my son had the situation that preceded our move to Arizona from Chicago. Several boys were taking kids who were standing in line to leave school at the end of the day, throwing them on the floor, and roughing them up, presumably because they were trying to start their own gang. They threatened the kids they assaulted, telling them to not say anything—so, when it happened to my son, I didn't know about it until my mother learned about it from another boy she used to take to school.

> I would not allow my son to go to a school where there was no protection provided for their students.

When I went to the school to discuss the situation, they were unwilling to do anything. When I chose to move my son to another school, administrators there tried to talk me out of it, but I told them I would not allow my son to go to a school where there was no protection provided for their students.

There was another instance with my daughter when a girl was picking on her on the school bus. When I reported it, school officials said that the next time my daughter and the other girl had a problem, they were going to remove both of them from the school bus. That was unacceptable. I depended on the bus to get my daughter to and from school. Whenever I had to go to the school, I found that if I tried to be nice, nothing would be done, but if I got angry and upset, that's when things happened. As I learned all of the different things going on from Gwen, I thought, *Oh, no. Here we go again. There are things going on in the schools and no one is doing anything. They are allowing kids to continue bullying other children.*

I went to a few of their meetings and met Janelle. I was appalled when I heard some of the stories. One scenario I remember had a biracial little boy in a class where a kid dared another kid to call him the "n" word. He did, and the biracial boy told the teacher, who said that was not going to be tolerated. Then another kid got involved and called the biracial boy a cotton-picker. That caused them to have a fight—but it was the biracial boy that ended up being suspended from school. There have been so many situations like that one where somebody else initiated the problem, but the victim ended up being the one kicked out of school. That should not be happening.

As a result, I now serve on Black Mothers Forum governing board—and I love serving under Janelle's leadership. She reminds me of Shirley Chisholm, the first Black woman to ever run for President of the United States. Through Black Mothers Forum, I've learned how advocacy and being a protector mesh together. We are trying to protect kids from being part of the school to prison pipeline as well as from unfair treatment and being bullied. We are constantly advocating for people in order to try to protect them.

I believe there are three ways Black mothers can best be a protector for their children and their families. First, we should be informed about what is going on in the classrooms with our kids. Children don't always share, and some parents don't always ask. We can't protect what we don't know. Are they being bullied in class? Is the instructor or teacher treating them in a respectful manner? We keep hearing horror stories about inappropriate touching of students from both men and women. That was never heard of when I was in school, but now it is happening more and more. I'll never forget when my granddaughters came home from school one afternoon and told me about a weird boy in their class who they said likes blood so much he admitted to drinking his sister's blood. They were only 11.

You've got to be engaged with your children so that they feel comfortable having those kinds of conversations with you. Otherwise, you'll never know what is going on. Set that expectation for engagement and establish that bond with your children as early as you can. Mothers definitely have to be more involved in the interests of their children, particularly involving their well-being while they are in the care of others. We need to know how they are doing mentally and emotionally.

Second, we should be knowledgeable about what to do in certain situations as well as how to go about doing it. We need to know who to contact and what steps to follow when there is an issue. Finally, we should be committed to stay in the fight for the long haul. Many mothers don't want to get involved because they don't want to go through it. It takes too much. They don't have the time. They can't take off work. They are too stressed. They are fearful because they don't know what the outcome is going to be, while their children are afraid because they don't want to be ostracized for coming home and telling their parents about what is going on. Kids deserve to be protected, but for some reason they don't feel like they deserve it. They believe they just have to go through whatever it is, but they don't have to.

As a result of all of this, I hear, "I can't" a lot—but in many cases, we are the *only* protector our children and families have. They need us to be their Underdog and fight for them as their Wonder Woman.

We can—and we must—be their protector.

CHAPTER 3

—

RESOURCEFUL RESILIENCE:
Making Strategic Moves

"I am able to do all things through Him who strengthens me."
~ Philippians 4:13

I am often in awe of the many challenges and adversities Black mothers have overcome throughout American history. We have collectively faced severe trials that had the potential to put us straight out of our minds, yet we still rise. I am simply amazed at how our foremothers took the discouragements, terror, insults, beatings, sexual assaults, as well as the stripping away of their children and their husbands, and still used what they had to cook a meal, clothe themselves, stand in cotton fields, nurse babies, and make the best of dirt floors and cold nights.

They did it all in the hope that life would be better for their children if only they could just hold on.

That is the brilliant resourceful resilience of the Black mother.

A resourceful person has the ability to effectively move with creativity to wisely and efficiently use the information and resources available to accomplish something. She has the mindset that says, "I will figure this out." A resilient person has the ability to recover their strength, determination, spirit, flexibility, and sense of humor in the midst of adversity, discouragement, disappointment, mistakes, trials, and tribulations. She has the mindset that says, "The only thing that beats failure is to try, so I will keep on trying."

The resourceful, resilient Black mother has developed the capacity to manage complex situations efficiently, appropriately, and with the emotional capacity to see things through to their expected end. She has learned to adapt well in the face of significant sources of stress such as trauma, tragedy, or threats. Intentionally or not, we have developed this resourceful resilience, as did our foremothers, to raise up the next generation of Black mothers.

Our level of response to the many uncomfortable circumstances we find ourselves in on a daily basis has mandated us to take advantage of all our capabilities through balance, reason, logic, and emotion instead of through an explosive emotional response that only exacerbates the situation. Nothing is accomplished when that happens, yet many of our mothers have overlooked the value of their emotional capacity because things happen so fast, we often do not have an opportunity to adequately assess our emotional well-being to handle yet another crisis or confrontational event.

As a result, mental health is a significant problem in our community, and it has a historical precedent. Our foremothers never had an opportunity to get mental health counseling for their extremely stressful and traumatic situations, nor did they have the opportunity to have their emotional wellness tanks refilled. So, generation after generation, we as Black mothers have been told we need to just "shake it off" or "deal with it," stuffing things down deep within us so we can keep moving. Black mothers don't have the time, or the luxury, to address how we feel or process what is happening, so our emotional capacity is often minimal at best. The "angry Black mother" is the inevitable result of this reality.

Thankfully, mothers who do address and process what has happened to them and have been afforded the opportunity to get mental health counseling and spiritual renewal have a more balanced lifestyle, resulting in their emotional capacity being at a more mature level. They can withstand more and are able to respond in even, thoughtful, and proactive ways to achieve their intended outcomes.

———

How do we as Black mothers expand our resourceful resilience? There is a mother I know who has exercised both better than anyone else I've ever met. Debora Colbert-Green has been instrumental in identifying resources to help in our efforts at Black Mothers Forum to create safe and supportive learning environments for our children. Debora was the one who brought the concept of microschools to my attention as a potential learning model, bringing us one step closer to ending the school to prison pipeline. In addition, Debora has been an integral part in equipping us to build a platform where our children, parents, and educators have an opportunity to thrive in their educational endeavors.

Debora truly exemplifies what resourceful resilience looks like in the midst of trauma and uncertainty—and it is my prayer that you will be inspired by her story.

DEBORA COLBERT-GREEN
Written October 2021

The school was a quality one—Illinois Wesleyan University. Out of its 1,800 students that semester, I was one of only 20 Black pupils on campus. Because of my academic achievements in high school and earlier, I was enrolled as a freshman in a 300-level physiology class normally attended by juniors and seniors.

Yet at the end of my first day in that class, my professor asked, "Miss Smith, are you sure you're in the right place?"

Here we go again, I mused.

I'd heard the same exact question before, back in a high school mathematics class, and the query was given this time for the same reason it had years earlier. As a Black woman, my presence in a college classroom offering a higher-level course was thought to be a mistake. I couldn't possibly be smart enough.

It took a fresh surge of patience and resilience to assure the professor after class that my schedule confirmed I was precisely where I was supposed to be.

But that wasn't the worst of it. As the semester progressed. I'll never forget the day when the professor asked the class,

> Being the only Black person of the dozen or so students in the class, everybody wondered how I was going to react.

"Do you think that the size of the brain in a Black person is smaller than the size of a brain in White people?"

A hush enveloped the room. Being the only Black person of the dozen or so students in the class, everybody seemed frozen in time as they wondered how I was going to react. The looks on their faces ranged from empathy and sympathy to those who rolled their eyes in amazed exasperation. That was understandable. By then, I had established myself as someone the professor and students could turn to for answers and insights. Still, I struggled to suppress my shock that such a question could even be posed, much less considered, at a so-called institution of higher learning.

Knowing that college is a place where everyone should be able to spread their wings and be free to speak the way they feel, I took a deep breath—and explained why that question was ridiculous and how there was no evidence to support such an outlandish and degrading claim. I named all of the Black inventors and scientists who had created everything from the clothes they wore to the air conditioning that cooled our classroom. To conclude, I reminded everyone, "I am not here to teach. I am here to learn. I hope I'll never again be asked a question like that because there is absolutely no scientific proof to substantiate it."

Later, some of my classmates told me they had never heard about the many Black contributions that I mentioned. Others would ask me to join study groups with them, invite me out for a meal, or to attend campus functions and parties.

Not so with the professor, however, who asked me to stay after class. I could tell he did not like what I had said by the way his body literally changed color. His pigment morphed to a nice, bright red, so I assessed that he was likely both embarrassed and upset by my response to the ridiculousness of his question.

When we were alone, however, he stubbornly stood by what he said—and he continued to ask me how I got into the class to begin with. Several individuals had already suggested to me that the only reason that I was there was because I was Black, not because I had earned it with the full-ride academic scholarship I gained. They were convinced I was at the university because of affirmative action, not my brain.

I would have changed classes if I could. But it was a small university, and there weren't a lot of choices. When I finally escaped from the professor, I diligently searched for a safe place where I could sit and cry. As I began to wonder if Illinois Wesleyan was the right place for me, it hit me that I had to figure out how to stay there while remembering, as a Black person, that my family had experienced such warped thinking for generations. I could not believe this was what I had to face, but I had to be resilient and strong enough to deal with it.

That happened in 1975—and in many ways, it seems little has changed since then in America, not just for Black women, but for all disenfranchised or marginalized groups. That is why possessing the *resilience* to have strong conviction, determination, and internal motivation to create a plan, stick to it, and keep your faith while overcoming adversity is so important, heeding that inner voice that tells you, "Yes, I can ... Yes, I will ... Do it!"

That's what I did back in college. During that time, Black Power was the mantra of the day. Having pride, understanding who I was, and knowing what my parents had instilled in me, along with what had been accomplished in the civil rights movement, allowed me to be resilient.

But it was good to get some help. There were only two Black professors on campus, one in English and humanities and the other in the science department. The safe place I happened upon that day was the classroom of Dr. Frank Starkey. He was preparing for a chemistry class when I came in and broke down in tears.

He and I talked about what had just happened, and he assured me, "That is not okay. That is not acceptable. I will be talking to my colleague, but the one thing I would like to do is to become your mentor."

From that moment forward, Dr. Starkey and I became friends and allies. He guided me through my time and my studies at the university, and he helped me to realize that I wanted to change my major from pre-med to behavioral science. Thanks to his mentoring, I felt safe and finally supported in what seemed like a foreign land. That was one of the best things I could have experienced, for I realized I *was* worthy.

I *did* deserve to be there.

I could *perform* in that arena.

I went on to lead and stage a sit-in to fight for a Black student union and a Black house on campus because everybody else had a retreat or refuge while Black students did not. I started organizing, meeting with both the dean and the president of the university, stating my position on why we were doing what we were doing. I was resilient.

———

I grew up in the Chicago area, one of the most segregated cities in America, but I did not grow up poor. My grandparents and parents had the resources to live in communities where Blacks were either not welcome or not present at all. That allowed me to go to school with a lot of White people and be involved in educational experiences, such as mathematics and the sciences, that most Black people did not.

During high school, therefore, I was able to take part in summer programs at different universities such as Northwestern and Indiana State. The latter, in Terre Haute, Indiana, was challenging. My parents were very afraid of me going there because several spots in Indiana were a mecca for the Ku Klux Klan. No one accompanied me. My parents were in angst, but my mother,

Claricy Jeanette, always told me that old saying, "When someone hands you lemons, make lemonade." My sister tells me I am so much like my mother in how I want everyone to get along, love one another, and keep family close even when that can sometimes be challenging and contentious in its own right. I needed to be resilient not only in terms of my relationships and my family, but in staying committed to being a part of Indiana State's Honor Science Program, as the only Black kid in the science series, because I wanted to experience what it was like to do cell centrifugation at such a young age.

While there, I met a young lady named Rhea. She was from New York City, and we clicked because we both came from urban centers. I was cautious about going out in public, but she didn't understand.

"Let's go get a shake and a burger!" she said.

"Maybe I should just stay close and eat a peanut butter sandwich or something."

"No," she insisted, "we're gonna go out!"

I then proceeded to explain to Rhea my concerns and my parents' fears, and in her own way, she convinced me that I would be okay, and I was. As the program continued, both she and others started to learn and understand from me what it was like to be a Black person in that setting. They didn't realize the sense of fear and extra effort required for me to stay safe because there were people who didn't think I deserved to be there simply because of the color of my skin. Being able to excel, and even make friends with individuals from other cities, was wonderful and inspirational.

Such resilience carried me through high school and propelled me later during my college achievements and challenges. It continues to push me onward today as a retired corporate leader, business owner, executive director, advisor to a United States

Congressional leader, board chair, and university facilitator. I graduated and entered the corporate world in the 1980s during an era of affirmative action. That meant I had to constantly show the resilience to defend myself as someone who deserved promotion as opposed to being advanced only because I hit the three marks of being Black, being a woman, and being in leadership.

My first leadership opportunity was one of the hardest assignments I could have received. I had to lead people with whom I used to sit side-by-side as equals, and that could have put a wedge between me and them as they questioned if I really cared about them or had simply used them to catapult myself into that position of authority. I was able to gain their trust, create team cohesiveness, and thrive in that role because there were enough people there who really cared about me and were genuine in wanting to see me succeed. During my time in a male-dominated field at the number one insurance company in the United States, I always took on assignments that were unique or that no one had ever done, and I was eager to start new teams, launch new initiatives, and identify new ways to serve customers better. I also challenged the company to be more diverse in its customer base as well as in its professional and management ranks.

Throughout over 35 years in Corporate America, I believed that my responsibility as a leader was to help other people recognize their resilience, whether they came from a cultural or economic background that didn't allow them to believe in themselves or were in a situation where they had to overcome toxic dysfunction. I also assisted individuals who were part of the gay community, well before they achieved civil rights status, to safely navigate the corporate environment, and I educated people in and around that community about AIDS (acquired immunodeficiency syndrome) after HIV (human immunodeficiency virus) arrived in the country in 1981. There were also people who started with the company who had only a high school diploma, and I encouraged and mentored 200-plus women and men through higher learning. Many went on to get bachelor's degrees, master's degrees, and PhDs.

> It is very important to me that people be respected, have a sense of belonging, and benefit from inclusivity.

Right before I retired, I received over 2,000 emails from people all across the company, expressing to me how I had touched their lives in a positive manner—from answering a question or guiding them through the steps to apply for a job to being there for the birth of their children. I went through a lot of tissues to get through all of those incredible email messages, and I got a thrill from watching people achieve things they never thought they could achieve. Then and today, it is very important to me that people be respected, have a sense of belonging, and benefit from inclusivity where they have equal access to opportunities and resources.

Yet I've discovered that resilience must be accompanied by something else that is just as vital: *resourcefulness*. Working and living in communities rich with resources, while seeing my sisters struggle to get the bare necessities in communities that were lacking, has taught me to navigate, advocate, and assist mothers, families, and women. I help them find information, become connected with the right people to acquire food or clothing, and get educational opportunities, pursue promotions, and even receive meals and gifts so they can freely celebrate holidays with their children and families. All of that indicates and produces resourcefulness.

Through the Greater Bethel Community Organization, we started Adopt a Family 365, which allowed several people to take on working with families for an entire year. We were able to empower mothers and women to not only get higher paying jobs, but to take parenting and financial literacy classes. Most of them had never even had a bank account. Music is one of my loves, so I also directed choirs and presented performing arts and plays for children and adults. On one occasion, I helped to bring together a group of people from around the community to play instruments and be in a choir. The ensemble performed for my entire company, and all the employees came out and looked down from all the floors as the group played and sang in the main corridor. We had a fantastic time.

As of this writing, I am 64 years of age, and my first and second grade teacher, Palace McCutchen, is still in my life. She was one of those people who saw something unique or different within me, embraced me because they have gone through the struggles themselves, and encouraged me to be and do what I was gifted to achieve. So, I want to be that same kind of woman in the lives of others—and I do it by first asking the right questions. The right question will usually lead to more resources and the ability to find those resources. I also strive to build multi-generational relationships outside of the Black community, and across cultures, to help others get the help they need. If that fails, I seek people who want to partner or collaborate to find a way to create the required resources.

Finally, I serve as a mentor to individuals and families. For example, I've spent nearly 20 years serving the Matthews family. I hired the big sister, Tracy, from a support position and promoted her to a professional level. I could see the potential in her that others could not. Her middle sister, Sherre, was not sure of her gifts or her goals, so I dedicated time with her to help with self-awareness and discovering her strengths. It emerged that her main strength was helping others to cope in difficult times and endure crises. At first, she did not see herself doing that, so I recommended that she do an internship. She did, and it led to her getting both bachelor's and master's degrees in that profession. With the next youngest sister, Pookie, I realized that her passion was creative beauty. A free spirit, she was a talented young woman as a hairstylist and as a musician who could hear a song and play it instantly on her flute. Finally, the baby sister, Kahla, was in middle school when I first met and mentored her. I had her create a vision board of all her dreams and possibilities. Not only did she pursue her passion in dancing and performing arts, but she is loving it.

All four, Tracy, Sherre, Pookie, and Kahla, came from a family where college was just a notion and where achieving high paid professional jobs was a dream. They had never experienced, or even thought about, the possibility of getting a degree, much less getting four degrees. Their family now values learning as a lifetime mission. Being able to mentor, guide, and assist them by providing encouragement, a safe place, and challenging work allowed them to achieve their goals. To see each of them today as homeowners, and as individuals who assist in the community, is so rewarding, and I can call on them at any time, confident they will provide their time and effort.

As my upbringing attests, I do not know what it is like to be poor. Working and living in communities rich in resources has been the story of my life. Knowing that those communities had everything anyone needed within walking distance or a bike ride told me that all things are possible—so why can't everybody have access to the things they need? Is it that they don't want access, or is it that there are actually systems in place that keep people from getting that access?

It turns out it's a combination of the two, depending on the person. Those who have gone through cycles, or generations, of trauma and hardship without getting any help have learned to survive any way they can. That is not a judgment. It is an *act of living* that they have grown accustomed to in the many deprived communities of America. It takes resourcefulness to help those who have never imagined the possibilities to break free of that reality by providing relevant learning materials and identifying different ways of communicating within their families where angry expression and hurtful words are common.

I worked with a family that had two sons in their late teens. One was a self-starter; the other needed a lot of attention. The parents had always compared the two, and that created dissention both in terms of how they communicated with one another and in their relationship with their mother and father. I focused everyone on not only interacting with each other in new ways, but also on how to allow the sons to express and embrace their individual dreams without negative comparison. It took about six months, but we progressed to where the sons broke free and found their identity. One son pursued engineering and the other became an artist. Meanwhile, their parents, who had worked so hard to provide the financial and material resources for their family, realized they had overlooked the emotional resources their boys required. Complicating matters was the fact that the son who became an engineer was a homosexual, and this was a point of contention for the parents. I was able to help them deal with and accept their son so that he could express himself without judgment. This brought everyone together to create unity.

The other thing I have done over the last several years, especially with Black Mothers Forum, is to work with mothers, grandmothers, and caregivers who are working with the foster care system—a difficult experience for everyone involved. I have helped them through advocacy by assisting them to develop a plan and connecting them to organizations that can help them get their families back together. As they are more educated about the various services and systems, their level of confidence grows. Their personal ownership increases, and the blaming of others diminishes, which leads to breaking the cycle of anger and broken homes. Becoming better parents means becoming better women and men with a deeper understanding of how their own experiences have impacted them as adults and parents.

It has been both a joy and a privilege to advocate for and assist mothers and their families to be resilient and resourceful. One woman that comes to mind is Pat, a single mother who believed she could never own her own home. Pat came from a family where two generations had lived in the projects. Her grandmother was no longer married, her mother was single, and Pat herself was a single mother with four children. An extremely bright young lady, Pat had a high school diploma, but she was in a low paying job and did not have a bank account.

I saw something in Pat that told me she could achieve more, and I connected her with Habitat for Humanity. As she went to work with that organization to put in the sweat equity to help build her own home, I helped Pat get a better job so that she could open a bank account and set aside money to maintain and furnish the home. Little did she know, though, that I was secretly working with the community to furnish the home for her. Watching her beam with pride as she and her daughter turned the key on the door of their home was amazing enough, but their reaction to how intentionally we had furnished the home, especially her daughter's room, was incredible! Today, Pat's children are all grown, and her oldest child is purchasing her first home.

That is what it is like to break the cycle—and sometimes we have to embrace others so that they can do just that while fulfilling their dreams and passions.

In the work that I do as part of Black Mothers Forum, I help women from teens through senior citizens to navigate housing, everything from preventing them from eviction or purchasing their own home. I also assist them in understanding how to negotiate for a pay raise. One woman, Alyson, was working with a technology company as a human resources manager, and she was asked to train a new colleague to do the same work she did. In the course of working with me, we discovered that the colleague, a White male, was getting a starting pay that was $15,000 more than she was making after being at the company for a long time.

Women, particularly those of color, often have a fear of negotiating. For them, it equates to a fear of losing their job. I helped Alyson identify what she had contributed to the company, and I asked her how much she would like to earn. She said an additional $5,000, but I told her she should probably be earning $15,000 more than she was. She said she didn't think she would ever get that from this company. So, I conducted a 360 assessment with her through which we gained feedback from her colleagues, and we discovered there were many who said they would not have been able to achieve what they had without Alyson's influence. That was priceless.

I worked with her to better recognize her own accomplishments, and we role played together to prepare for the negotiation.

In the meantime, I had her apply to three other companies where the salary would be in line with what she felt she deserved. Two of those companies made offers, and one of them offered her more than she thought her current employer would be willing to pay. Armed with all that information and my coaching, Alyson went into negotiations with her company and received a better offer than she was originally going to request, but ultimately, she ended up going with the company that was going to pay her even more.

> The process taught her what her full value, potential, and worth actually was.

In the end, Alyson got so much more than monetary gain. She gained confidence in herself. She also realized that she didn't have to limit her capabilities to someone else's expectations of her. The process taught her what her full value, potential, and worth actually was.

Today, I think back to my great-grandfather, grandfather, and grandmother, all of whom I consider to be trailblazers who were ahead of their time. I try to imagine what my great-grandfather, Sandy Pruitt, must have gone through to own every acre of land that he worked as an indentured servant so that he could leave that land as a legacy to his family.

My grandfather, John Smith, who did not finish high school, was a master with his hands, making and repairing shoes. In the 1920s, he started his first business in Mississippi at a time when that was almost unheard of. Later, he moved north in the Great

Migration from the south and landed in Detroit. Things didn't work out the way he wanted there, so he picked up and took the family to Chicago, where he opened up not just one shoe shop, but three.

My grandmother, Linnie Ruth, was a hard-working person who started her life as a teacher in a one-room schoolhouse in Mississippi. Because of segregation, she taught kindergarten through twelfth grade in that schoolhouse. She was the voice that told her children and grandchildren about the importance of education and how it makes a person a resilient, resourceful, and viable contributor.

Each one of them have informed who I have become—yet there are so many women today who could make a difference in their communities and society but don't have that someone, or those someones, to encourage them. Prior to joining Black Mothers Forum in 2016, I oversaw a group of 45 girls ages nine to 17 and young women ranging in age from 18-24 called the Daughters of Destiny. Some of these young women are still in my life today, thriving as veterinarians, in robotics, or in engineering, achieving things people told them they would never be able to do.

Girls such as these, and Black people in general, need mentors who can serve them like a personal board of directors to guide them and advise them when they are not going in the right direction. They need mentors who care for them and do not criticize them. If you are in need of such a mentor, seek one. If you can become such a mentor, find a young woman who needs your support. Together, you will become resilient and resourceful enough to not only impact this generation, but to become the trailblazers for those to come.

CHAPTER 4

—

DETERMINATION:
Immovable and Steadfast

"Stand firm, and you will win life."
~ Luke 21:19

When it comes to being a Black mother, it all boils down to the determination she has to meet the needs of her family. She must be firm and resolute, unmoved by the barrage of obstacles she faces on a daily basis. This is something she has developed along the way, and she watches it play out in how she continues to wake up from one day to the next, staying engaged in this thing called "life" to make sure her family has everything they need. This determination is accompanied by a certain calm that allows her to hold steady to assure her sustainability in meeting those needs.

Often, we as Black mothers do not even realize that we are exhibiting this determination by not only surviving today's crisis, but by putting necessary protections in place to make sure it doesn't happen again and insulating our families from any future harm. The characteristics of our determination are seen, heard, and felt, and each one is activated at various times, especially as we take care of our children. There are certain characteristics many Black mothers have had to develop in order to remain immovable and steadfast in our fight to keep our children safe and alive. They are as follows:

Bravery acknowledges those situations, challenges, encounters, or dangerous people who cause us to be fearful so that, even in the face of these things, we have the ability to overcome and press on. One example that exemplifies bravery is how we, as a people, have continued to stand against institutional racism that we have had to deal with for over 400 years. This is oftentimes daunting and fearful, yet it is the right thing to do when it comes to creating safe and supportive environments for our children.

Confidence is a firm understanding of our personal and collective capabilities and limitations. As I think about Black mothers who have come before us who consistently exhibited this characteristic, Sojourner Truth and her famous speech "Ain't I a Woman?" comes to mind. She compared the amount of work she handled, the load she carried, the lashes she took, and the 13 children she birthed into this world as far greater and of more value than any man could ever claim during her time, and I would daresay, even today.

Decisiveness is knowing that we have a responsibility to assess our situation, decide the appropriate course of action, and move forward toward reaching our intended goals. Black mothers, especially single mothers, are faced with many decisions throughout the day as it relates to the well-being of their households. There are those who have to decide whether or not they will quit their job because they are being bullied or overlooked for a promotion. While keeping in mind they have a family depending on their income, they therefore must stand down, shut their mouths, and endure discriminatory practices in order to keep their jobs and continue to feed, clothe, and shelter their children. There are others who have decided to take a chance to follow their dreams and have provided far more for their children then they could have ever imagined. Cathy Hughes, founder of Radio One, was once homeless due to a failed marriage, but went on to pursue her dream in radio and television. Today, she is considered the second wealthiest Black mother in the nation.

Focus is one of our greatest struggles, but we must remain unphased by the external forces that can hinder our progress, and we must stay the course to reach our end goals. We have so many situations that we are navigating at once, we can be overwhelmed by the demands on our mind, heart, and time. I am challenged in this area on a daily basis, and I am constantly amazed at how much still gets done even when I don't believe I have accomplished a thing.

I have always been fascinated by women who seem to have it all together and make staying focused look like it is a breeze. Oprah Winfrey is a Black woman who has exhibited these characteristics without fail. She may not be a biological mother, but she has coached and mentored many young people who consider her like a mother. Oprah faced much discrimination and many financial challenges on her rise through the broadcasting ranks. It would have been easy for her to lose sight of her vision. Now, as a result of her focus, she is considered the queen of all media. Wow!

Once we fix our minds as Black mothers on the obstacles, challenges, or fears that exist, we take control of each situation, recognizing that it doesn't matter who is for us or against us. We are going to pursue it anyway—and it would be best for whoever is in our way to move before they *get* moved. When we set ourselves to the problem at hand, we will not rest until it is solved.

Nothing and no one can stop a determined mother from protecting her children.

I mean no one.

At Black Mothers Forum, we have spent countless hours meeting with women and their families to address the traumas they face at the hands of the police or school administrators, motivating them to stay the course and dismantle the impact of these oppressive systems. Speaking up for the fair and just treatment of our children has been both scary and liberating at the same time—and the need to keep standing, keep showing up, keep speaking, and keep moving shows that we are unwilling to accept the status quo that says children have to settle for what is being handed to them.

As I think about the Black mothers we have worked alongside, the ones who stand out are older mothers who have raised their families, helped raise other families, and are now in their grandparenting years. We can learn so much from our senior mothers if we are willing to stop and listen to them.

One such mother has determined to make sure our children's academic, social, emotional, and physical needs are met. I will let her introduce herself to you.

In Her Own Words

GWEN PAYTON
Written October 2021

I am a 71-year-old mother, grandmother, and great-grandmother. I am also a daughter, a sister, and a Black mother of four adult children, all of whom did well in public schools and never faced any problems in those schools.

So, you can understand my surprise and shock when I read *The New Jim Crow* by Michelle Alexander. A book detailing the mass incarceration of Black people, it was introduced to me when I took part in the same book club meeting that Janelle Wood attended—the meeting that ultimately led to the birth of Black Mothers Forum.

> Nothing and no one can stop a determined mother from protecting her children.

I had never even heard of the school to prison pipeline that has been used to criminalize the normal behaviors of Black children through school suspensions and expulsions so that they find themselves in situations that increase their chances of coming into contact with law enforcement. But once I had, I was appalled.

"These kids can't be that terrible." I said to myself. "What is going on?"

When Black Mothers Forum began, I became a charter member—and I started to find out exactly what *was* going on. At first, it was hard for me to relate. I had never experienced anything like it in school, even though I came of age in the late 1960s onward. My children had never experienced anything like it, either, and they had gone on to achieve incredible things. One daughter has a Ph.D. and is a college professor. One son has a bachelor's degree, and another has his master's degree. My other daughter worked in a corporate environment for over two decades. Not one of them had to deal with the school to prison pipeline.

But things have certainly changed, and not for the better. The number of Black men that are incarcerated, and the length of time for which they are incarcerated, is terrible. Black boys are far more likely to be suspended and kicked out of school than any of their counterparts: Brown, Native American, disabled, or White. I simply refuse to believe that Black boys have worse behavior than the rest of the kids.

Something is wrong—and I *have* to do something about it.

Today, I am a member of the board for Black Mothers Forum. I also serve as a guide in our microschool, meaning I am essentially a homeschool version of a teacher. I regularly attend school board meetings to address policies, curriculums, and practices that do not create a safe and supportive learning environment for our Black children, especially our Black sons.

As an older woman, I am determined to be involved and make a difference so that today's Black mothers can have the help and support they need to wage the battles they must in order to protect their children and their families.

I am immovable in my resolve and steadfast in my commitment, and I hope I can inspire other senior women to join me.

Our young Black women desperately need us.

Here are just three examples that will explain why.

A group of elementary school kids were playing a game of tag at recess. The game was not being played in a malicious way, but the teacher who observed the game said there was a strict no tolerance policy about hitting, no matter what the children were doing. All of the kids were written up—but the only child that got suspended was the Black youngster in the group.

A middle school girl, a mixed-race child, and her White friend were riding on the school bus. They always sat in the same seat, and a little boy, who probably liked one of them, sat behind them. He began poking both girls in the back of their heads. They got tired of it and told the driver, who stopped the bus, went back, and asked the boy to stop. The boy, who was White, cussed out the driver. After the bus was back on its way to the school, the boy resumed his behavior, and the two girls decided to retaliate.

A fight broke out in which the White girl pulled out some of the White boy's hair, and the driver reported the incident to the school principal. The boy was known to be a bully and had been in trouble before—but only the mixed-race girl was suspended from school and had to go to juvenile court.

When Black Mothers Forum, representing the girl's mother, went to the principal to find out why she was the only one suspended, I was told by the police officer that this mixed-race girl was the only one that showed up on the surveillance camera on the bus. I found that hard to believe. How could the camera only see her but not the boy or the other girl pulling his hair out?

Finally, we had to advocate on behalf of a high school freshman, a Black girl, was being verbally abused by white boys at her school, one was a freshman and his brother was a junior, they followed her around campus calling her the "n" word. Administrators told her to simply get a thicker skin. The older boy continued to provoke her and eventually took a swing towards her face, and a fight ensued. The police were called, and the school was shut down temporarily—but it was the Black girl who was ultimately suspended. The school district decided she was an imminent danger to the other students, and she was forced to finish out her freshman year online. To my knowledge, nothing was ever done to discipline the older boy who posed the real threat.

————

In every case, the mothers or grandmothers of these youngsters had to battle for their children's well-being in the face of injustice—and I have come to realize that such instances are becoming much more the norm than the exception in many of our schools. In light of this reality, one of the most important things older Black women can do is become a mentor to our younger Black sisters. Many of them are exhausted, and they need someone who will listen to them talk about their struggles.

When it comes to being *determined*, I would mentor a young woman to be present and involved in her children's lives, particularly their schooling. Show up for your children's parent-teacher conferences. If there is a conflict between you and the school over an issue such as what your children are learning, address it right away and decide what you can do to help your children and their teachers. Strive to come to an agreement where their teachers understand that you are available. Give the teachers your contact information. Even if you have a job where you don't have a lot of flexibility, let the teachers know that you want to be called if there is a need that requires you to come to the school. This way, they'll know that you are concerned.

When my oldest daughter was in high school, she always wore short shorts despite my objections. One day, one of her male teachers made a remark about her appearance, saying that he thought she looked like a "hooker." I was at work in a management training program when she told me what had happened, and even though I didn't want to miss any of the training, I knew I had to leave. I disagreed with what she was wearing, but I needed to be there for my daughter.

I met with the teacher, the assistant principal, and a school counselor, and I told them the teacher did not have the right to do what he did. "Even if she was violating the dress code," I said, "the remark was derogatory. You could have said, 'Young lady, you need to not wear those shorts,' or 'You need to dress more according to the dress code,' not that she looked like a hooker."

The teacher denied saying that, but I didn't believe my daughter was lying. "Don't say anything derogatory like that to my daughter ever again," I said, "and if there is anything she is doing that is not according to school rules, contact me first."

Thanks to my determination to defend my daughter, there was never another incident like that—and it was later, once my daughter had graduated and had started working, that she said she understood what I meant about people's perceptions and how she dressed.

I would also mentor a young woman to be *immovable* by teaching her that the time she spends with her children now is going to determine to a great extent her children's confidence in themselves. It will also show them how to resolve conflict. Your children will look to you to see if you are going to stick up for them and how you are going to do it. It is not going to be easy. You may not get the outcome you desire. But you want all parties involved to know that if anything ever happens again, you will be there and you will do everything you can to resolve the situation in your children's favor.

My youngest daughter was in a high school English class as part of her international baccalaureate courses, and they were reading a book in which a character was described as having "nigger eyes." My daughter told me it made her very upset, and I assured her I would talk to her English teacher about it. When I met with him, he was quite unapologetic. He said that he did not choose the books the school used, he wouldn't stop using the book, and that the book was "literature," so my daughter shouldn't be so upset—and neither should I. I reiterated that she was indeed upset before adding that the school never taught anything positive in the class about Black history. He replied that English was not a Black history class and that he wouldn't be teaching Black history in it.

We never came to an agreement. I would have preferred that the teacher provide an explanation to the whole class instead of just reading about "nigger eyes" and moving right along. It was clear to me that the other children were embarrassed to say anything, and they were embarrassed for my daughter. I thought he could have been more sensitive. But I was immovable because I would not be swayed from my opinion or from my right to declare it.

Finally, I would mentor a young woman to be *steadfast* by finding someone to walk alongside her as she deals with issues involving her children, particularly if she is single. Find advocates such as myself, an organization like Black Mothers Forum, or perhaps your church or a similar support group. You need another woman who can go with you to the school because it is very hard to hold your emotions down when you are by yourself. She can help you sit down, look at the facts, discover how the situation is affecting your children, and then come up with a remedy. It is vital that you view the issue in a matter-of-fact manner and give yourself time to consider what you will say. The school will have teachers, administrators, and even lawyers. If you go in alone, you can feel very vulnerable.

There was a situation where my youngest son, a talented high school basketball player, wanted to also participate in a debate competition that required him to miss one basketball practice to attend. The basketball coach, however, told him that was unacceptable, and that if he attended the competition, he'd be kicked off of the team. I thought that was unacceptable—so I tried to make an appointment to see the coach. When that went unanswered, I went to practice and waited until I could speak to the coach in person. I told him that my son was serious about basketball, and I didn't feel that missing one practice to go to the competition warranted penalizing my son in any way, much less removing him from the team. "My son is a great student. He is a great basketball player. It is very unfair of you to make him choose between basketball and the debate competition."

The coach was not happy and dismissed what I had to say. When I went to the school's administration, the principal agreed with the coach. I wasn't going to make my son miss the debate, and the coach did kick him off the team. My son didn't want that to happen and hoped that I could do something to change the situation, but he understood the debate was important as well.

My steadfastness would pay off. A collegiate coach who had seen my son play offered him a scholarship at a small local college. My son went on from there to earn an athletic scholarship to a Division One school where he played basketball and earned his college degree.

I encourage you, especially if you are a senior Black woman, to get involved in other ways as well. Please attend school board meetings, and if you are healthy enough, run for seats on the school board. It is a great place to help make decisions that benefit your children. At most of the school board meetings I have attended, there were few to no people of color present, despite the fact that these meetings are open to parents and concerned citizens. In addition, look into your state's legislature. Go online and ask questions. Examine the laws that are on the books and challenge anything you do not agree with. Find out what is coming up on the docket and make yourself available for the sessions virtually or in person. With either of these involvement options, you need to be in for the long haul. Dig in, be steadfast, and don't budge.

As an older Black woman, I am encouraged by young people. They are bold. They have an opinion, and they don't mind telling anyone what their opinion is. However, they don't always know how to express themselves in a way they can be more effectively heard. For instance, I've been at school board meetings where young people got up, made a big commotion, and drowned things out so the meeting couldn't proceed. It disrupted the board from doing something the young people disagreed with, but it didn't stop them. As older people, we need to gain their confidence so they will trust us to show them *how* to best be heard. That said, the fact that they are bold enough to state what they believe in, what they want, and follow through the best they know how is inspiring to me.

As I enter into the twilight years of my life, I remain optimistic about what I can achieve. First and foremost, I want to enjoy my family, but I also desire to be a resource for young people, sharing with them my experiences and any expertise they might need. I want to be of service to them and uplift them in whatever ways that I can, so they can leave an enduring legacy on their families and in their communities. As I do, I plan to stay active for as long as I can and enjoy my children, grandchildren, and great-grandchildren.

I have enjoyed my life. I am pleased with what I have accomplished so far—but I am not done yet. There is still more to do, and I will be steadfast to see it through.

CHAPTER 5

LEADERSHIP COURAGE:
Truth to Power

"My words are from the integrity of my heart,
And my lips speak knowledge sincerely.
~ Job 33:3, NASB

It is safe to say that our society is starving for leaders who possess the courage to have the necessary conversations to address the laws, policies, practices, and mindsets that have a harmful impact on the well-being of our Black families. These leaders do not care if they will be alienated or ostracized for speaking the truth to those in positions of authority who have the power to make the necessary adjustments to stop the harm.

There are people who believe that if someone holds a particular position, has a certain title, or earns a large salary, they are a leader. But I have discovered, particularly through the work I do with Black Mothers Forum, that many of those who have such positions, titles, or salaries are not leaders at all. They are just taking up space and eating up time.

Rather, a true leader is someone who can actually move people toward a common cause or solution. A true leader says and does what is required to benefit the people they serve. True leaders recognize that the authority they have is to be used solely for the uplifting of their respective communities. True leaders demonstrate courage in the face of fearful and harmful situations.

Therefore, true leadership courage comes from those who seek truth and wield power with integrity, self-awareness, empathy, and gratitude while showing the ability to communicate, delegate, learn, and influence. Black mothers exhibit this leadership courage. We have integrity because our families depend on us to do what we say we are going to do. We must operate in such a way that garners the trust of our families and looks out for the well-being of our communities. Our children must trust that what we do and say is above reproach.

Black mothers have self-awareness because we must know ourselves so we can teach our children how to be the best persons they can be. We will do this only if we model behaviors and make decisions that show them how to be their best. Black mothers are empathetic, enabling us to nurture others while pushing them to be all they were created to be, whether it be a great orator, ballerina, doctor, professional, engineer, or even the President of the United States. As Black mothers, we show gratitude to others because we have discovered thankfulness goes a long way in raising up young adults who are gracious, respectful, and willing to serve others.

Black mothers communicate in such a way that it does not demean, threaten, intimidate, or judge. This tone of nurturing, loving care is especially critical for the mental and emotional well-being of our children. As Black mothers, our ability to delegate is much easier when our families see us do it first, coupled with a demonstration of how to get it, whatever "it" is for them.

Black mothers are teachable, and we learn because we know that when our children see us reading, taking classes, and willing to try new things, we demonstrate the importance of being life-long learners to them. Finally, Black mothers have influence in the way we challenge oppressive systems and garner the support of others to do the same, helping foster a better tomorrow for our children that is filled with hope and limitless opportunities to grow to their full potential and realize their true selves.

All of these characteristics manifest themselves in Black mothers as we display leadership courage in the face of pain and grief on a daily basis. For centuries, Black mothers have protected their children and families from belittling gestures, racism, abuse, sexual assault, incarcerations, lost employment, homelessness, and heartbreak such as the tragic and sometimes unnecessary deaths of our loved ones. There are countless mothers who go unnamed and unnoticed yet press onward and upward each day. Only a Black mother can stand up to a person in authority and speak to the grievances and wrongs their children have had to endure and not blink an eye—and when she takes on that bully called injustice, it's best to get out of her way.

> When she takes on that bully called injustice, it's best to get out of her way.

She will not be stopped or swayed by idle threats.

She will be heard.

She will not mince her words.

There will be no need to ask for clarification, for she will declare exactly what needs to be done to resolve the situation, and she will settle for nothing less than an immediate response. There will be no peace until the resolution meets her satisfaction.

JANELLE WOOD
Written November 2021

As a Black mother, I've had to go there for the sons and daughters of many Black families as well as for my own son, Bryce. I recall when he was in tenth grade. He was one of the star wide receivers on the football team at his high school in Phoenix, Arizona. On the afternoon of their homecoming game, the father of another student came to the campus drunk, wanting to pick up his daughter from school. As a result, the school administration would not release his daughter into his custody.

After he left the office, upset that the school administrators would not allow him to pick up his daughter, he actually pulled out of the parking lot and drove his car into the student areas of campus in search of his daughter—and my son happened to be standing in the path of his oncoming vehicle. Bryce's back was turned, making him unaware of the impending danger, and if it hadn't been for his girlfriend pulling him out of harm's way, the man would have killed him. The tire tread tracks of his truck ran over the back of my son's flip-flops. That was how close Bryce came to losing his life that day.

School officials, though, decided it wasn't worth the trouble to call and let me know what had happened. Instead, I found out about the incident from his girlfriend's mother, who happened to be sitting near me in the stands at the homecoming game that night.

"What a day!" she said, approaching me.

"What do you mean?" I asked.

"Bryce didn't tell you?"

"Tell me what?" I replied.

"He almost got hit by a drunk driver on campus today."

"What?" I exclaimed—and she went on to tell me what had happened. She concluded, "It was homecoming, and they told him to just shake it off because he had a game to play."

I was incensed. They were devaluing my child's life for a football game and a win.

Of course, the principal heard from Mama that Monday upon their return to school. I most definitely dealt with her, letting her know that I was going to report her to the district for blatant negligence and the reckless manner with which the entire incident was handled. I also demanded an apology for my son, which he was given.

We let Bryce finish out the semester, but we then withdrew him and moved him to another school with a much better reputation for creating a safe, supportive learning environment for Black males, a high school in Chandler, Arizona.

It is uncomfortable to enter into this leadership courage space as Black mothers, but enter it, we must. It is up to us to make sure our children have what they need—physically, academically, mentally, emotionally, socially, financially, and spiritually—and to clear the way for them to succeed and thrive regardless of what or who comes against them.

I remember when Black Mothers Forum was approached in 2018 by the principal at one of our Phoenix area schools because they were struggling with a high volume of suspensions or expulsions of their Black students, who made up one-fourth of the student population and some of whom were refugees, predominantly from Somalia. The principal called us in to address parents who were contentious and combative toward her and her predominately White staff. She had long meetings with these parents but seemed to be getting little results.

We scheduled a time to meet with those Black parents and their children and had about 30 families show up. In the meeting, we gathered qualitative data from those parents and students to identify their expectations and heard their concerns about the teachers and administration at the school. We found that there was a lack of upfront communication with the parents. For example, when a student exhibited behaviors contrary to what the teachers expected, it was not brought to the attention of the parent at the onset of that behavior. Instead, the teachers waited until they were so frustrated that they sent the child to the office with a referral that subsequently resulted in their suspension or expulsion.

The situation was challenging because the principal did not realize that the parent's expectations of her staff were different from the expectations the staff had for themselves. The parents required more nurture, authenticity, patience, and validation of their feelings, power, and abilities. They expected teachers to be forthcoming and patient with their children, and they wanted teachers to validate their children's feelings and level the playing field so that both children and parents had the same degree of power that they did. The teaching staff, however, felt it was the parents' responsibility to provide more discipline for their children, to make sure the students took care of their homework, and to assure that their children respected the teachers enough so that whatever the teachers said was considered valid without seeking clarification of their instructions. They also believed there was very little need for parents to question teachers. They had the mindset that the teachers knew best, and the parents had to fall in line.

When we shared this with the principal, it created tension between the principal and her lead teachers. Those teachers struggled with the fact that myself and other Black mothers were sharing this information with the principal, and that the principal was actually looking to make some changes in how the teaching staff conducted themselves with families of color. In the end, the principal made the changes, but she also lost some of her teaching staff who did not want to alter their behavior to better accommodate the expectations and needs of the students and parents they were there to serve and educate.

In another incident, I needed to confront the school superintendent of one of the Phoenix area's East Valley school districts serving students in kindergarten through eighth grade. At issue was a pattern of racial bullying and discriminatory disciplinary practices at one particular school in the district. I often found myself in the superintendent's office surrounded by other associate superintendents who came with the intention of intimidating me with their titles, their credentials, and their so-called data supporting their contention that there was no bullying or discrimination occurring at the school.

They were defensive and spoke to me in a condescending manner. I had to promptly state that, while I may not be considered an educator in their eyes, I was well educated, I could read, and I did recognize that the data they were showing me was outdated and didn't accurately reflect what was going on at the current time. In order to support my claim that many of our Black students were being racially bullied and disproportionately disciplined at a higher rate than their White peers within the district, I had to encourage teachers, staff, and parents to come forth anonymously via email or letters or agree to meet with me in undisclosed locations where I could gather this information. Once that data was collected, I was able to provide the superintendent with the necessary documentation to define the realities of the disproportionate disciplinary practices being exhibited within their school district.

As a result of our efforts, the superintendent put aside a sizeable amount of money to hire an equity consultant and create community and parent equity and inclusion counsels. It took about four to six months of pushing for change and providing the data required before the superintendent could move forward with a plan to provide more equitable solutions for children of color. Many hours and nights were spent sharing our findings at governing board meetings as well as with the school community.

———

In addition to our efforts with school administrators on behalf of Black parents and students, Black Mothers Forum also helps Black mothers use the leadership courage they already possess with their families and in their communities. In one instance, the daughter of one of our Black mothers was suspended and subsequently expelled during her freshman year of high school after she was arrested for fighting a boy who was two years older than her. The boy was one of two male students who were racially bullying and ridiculing her because of her color and her height. The boys had been calling her names when she approached one of her teachers to make the boys stop. However, the teacher told her she was being overly sensitive and to disregard the ridicule and bullying.

Being the leader that she is, and with little to no school administrative support, she decided to approach the boys outside of class and tell them to leave her alone. In response, one of the boys got his older brother and his brother's friends and encouraged them to begin intimidating and threatening her during school breaks and passing periods. Shortly after that, as she was trying to go to the cafeteria for lunch, one of the older boys cornered her and had words with her. She tried to make them stop and went into the lunchroom to avoid them, but the boy followed her, got in her face, and attempted to punch her. A big fight ensued, and she beat him up.

The school was placed on lockdown for a riot, the police were called, and school officials maintained that the riot resulted from her fighting back against the boy. She was detained in the school office without her mother being given the opportunity to speak to her, even after she requested that her mother be present. She was questioned without a parent or legal counsel there and then taken to the police department. Only then was her mother able to pick her up.

This mother didn't want any trouble. She had just gotten a new job and really wanted the entire situation to go away. I pushed her to press in about how her daughter had been treated, telling her that it was unfair for her daughter to be suspended because her daughter did not start the fight. In fact, school officials actually allowed the boy who started the fight to be dismissed from the premises, saying that he was injured. Meanwhile, the girl who was being bullied was forced to write a statement about the incident before anyone would allow her to contact her mother, again, even after she requested her mother's presence multiple times prior to being forced to write her statement. This is a classic example of the disparate treatment of Black children compared to their White peers.

I educated her mother on both her rights and her daughter's rights, and Black Mothers Forum also brought in other leaders in her community to help her. We enlisted their support, as well as that from other organizations, to help them understand the seriousness of the matter. The school was planning to expel the girl, and we had to attend a due process hearing. Because the mother could not afford an attorney, I had to prepare her to defend and advocate for herself, and I went into the hearing with her and provided counsel. She did a really good job of speaking up for her child and pointing out the facts of the disparate treatment between her daughter and the young man who actually started the fight.

Unfortunately, the hearing officer, who was hired by the district, decided in favor of expulsion, so we appealed the ruling and took it to a special session of the district's governing board. Again, the mother did not want to speak in front of the board, but I was able to encourage her, give her the tools she needed, and help her feel confident that her advocacy for her daughter was going to be beneficial in the end.

It did not turn out the way we wanted, and the girl was expelled for an entire school year—but the whole experience showed the girl that her mother was willing to stand up for her. The incident drew mother and daughter closer together than they had ever been before, and the mother gained courage that she didn't have before.

———

There's no doubt that Black mothers who do not feel capable of being courageous leaders can overcome that mindset. When they are armed with knowledge and information, it gives mothers support and, potentially, a way to reach the resolutions that they hope for. That gives them a tremendous amount of strength to stand up for what they believe in, even if it results in an outcome other than the one that they desired. I believe just getting our Black mothers to that point is the most beneficial thing in the world. It provides an opportunity for her to express her whole self in a situation where she has nothing else to lose, which is quite invigorating, empowering, and edifying. It is a huge confidence booster. Then, the next time something happens (and there is, sadly, almost always a next time for Black mothers with their children), they are less hesitant to step up to the plate and address the matter.

Be the Black mother you were called to be and the courageous leader your children need you to be. Let them see you standing up for what is right, no matter the cost, and free from concern about what others might say or think about you. You are a force to be reckoned with, and you will no longer be silenced.

CHAPTER 6

WISDOM:
Wise Counselor

*"An intelligent heart acquires knowledge,
and the ear of the wise seeks knowledge."*
~ Proverbs 18:15, ESV

A wise person once said that it is better to sit under the counsel of the wise than to be in the company of fools. More often than not, we find ourselves in the company of fools who would not necessarily identify themselves as being foolish. Even more troubling is that many of us don't realize those in our company are actually fools to begin with.

There's no doubt that we have oftentimes found ourselves lacking the knowledge we need to make the significant life decisions that will yield positive results for ourselves and for our families. At Black Mothers Forum, we have found that many of our mothers find themselves in situations where they are making choices based on limited information and with very little time to locate the details that they need to make an intelligent choice for themselves and their families. The continued destabilization of their mental, emotional, physical, and financial well-being is the result. Our mothers usually do not have access to wise counselors. Therefore, they are forced to move in directions where they neither have the guidance, knowledge, nor expertise to navigate.

I have had the privilege to meet many Black mothers from various walks of life, and in various seasons of life, who are experiencing the greatest challenges of their lives. Many of them need wise counselors with access to information, resources, and advice to help them—so it is imperative that Black mothers develop relationships with wise women and solicit their expertise when making significant decisions that will impact their families for generations to come.

I've had the blessing and the pleasure of working with many Black mothers who consider themselves wise and who are accessible to our mothers in need of wise counsel. One such mother who has walked alongside me in this quest is Debora Colbert-Green. Debora has had the opportunity to serve in many spaces where her experience in navigating difficult systems has proven to be an invaluable asset to our organization and the mothers in our community.

She and I have some words of wisdom we'd like to share with you.

In Their Own Words

JANELLE WOOD AND DEBORA COLBERT-GREEN
Written January 2022

The first time we saw one another was in 2014. Debora was the keynote speaker for the National Council of Negro Women, and Janelle was running for governor in the state of Arizona.

We didn't get a chance to speak to one another that day, but as Debora moved around the tables and visited with everybody, she thought it was fascinating that there was a Black woman running as a write-in candidate for the state's highest political office. She mentioned that very thing to some of those in attendance, and they shared with her how they knew Janelle from her work in the Phoenix community.

In the end, Janelle was unsuccessful in her attempt to secure the Americans Elect Party nomination in the August 26 primary, but that initial meeting would lead to others for the two of us. Debora was leading a group known as the Constellation that partnered with an organization called Demand to Learn. They were putting together information about school expulsion rates for our Black children. One of the main things she was working on was pinpointing who knew what was happening, who could do something about it, and how it could be done. In addition, as a corporate leader, Debora was connecting with different educational systems in several states and was disturbed that education was always being declared important but was being treated as if it was a fifteenth-class citizen. At the same time, Janelle was advocating for children who were being disciplined disproportionately and unfairly in an effort to end the school to prison pipeline.

It is amazing how our hearts, minds, passions, and personalities come together and balance one another.

Our paths constantly crossed in the work we were doing and the people we were seeing, and Debora invited Janelle to a Constellation meeting. As we began meeting and talking, we realized we had the same vision in a variety of areas—and a partnership began that has since secured and grown the ongoing work of Black Mothers Forum.

It is amazing how our hearts, minds, passions, and personalities come together and balance one another. Janelle allows Debora to step back and be who she is, which then allows Janelle to step in front and be who she is. Janelle enjoys talking to people about the issues at hand, while Debora's patient role is to say, "You know what the issue is. Let's go to work."

Debora likes to think big and put big ideas on the table, and she is able to present a vision in different ways (verbally, visually, or through step-by-step processes) so everyone can understand it and get behind it. Janelle likes to jump right in and swim. As Debora works strategically to figure out how to do things, taking us on a journey and asking the right questions to get us where we want to be, Janelle goes out and finds those individuals who are going to support the cause.

The way we work is like yin and yang. We know when we're not happy with each other, and that dynamic allows us to love one another yet make sure we stay focused on our passion to help Black mothers and their children. We came together out of our shared desire to help other people, show our compassion, and give—and for us to know that we have a friend who is a sister and a partner that we work with every day is tremendous.

Because of this symbiotic relationship, we have gleaned wisdom from one another in a variety of ways. For Debora, she has become wise in knowing when to follow. As someone who has been in a leadership role for many decades, Debora understands that it is hard for leaders to follow, but with Janelle she has discovered how to step back and say, "She has got this. Let her handle it in the way she needs to." In addition, Debora has discovered from Janelle how to bring out more empathy with certain people, but to temper it and discern where that person is at the moment. We both tend to give some people too much credit, so we can balance each other when we see that one or the other needs to be taken care of. Finally, Debora can be very reserved, tending to internalize some of the thoughts that she visualizes in a strategic setting. Janelle has taught her to open up and share, knowing that our wisdom is only as good as we apply it.

Janelle has learned wisdom from Debora by watching how she always has an elegance about her so that when she walks into a room, she shifts the atmosphere. She takes notice of how Debora conducts herself as she walks into a space. Debora has also helped Janelle learn how to comprehend massive amounts of information and content and sort through it at a rapid pace.

Because of how strategic Debora is about how to use information, Janelle has discovered how to process things in sequence in a way that gets people to where they need to be by slowing down and taking them on that journey. That has also taught Janelle that it is okay to take a break to self-reflect and self-discover to get her mind right. This allows her to refresh and renew as well as see a different perspective that she wouldn't have if she had simply rushed in.

The Bible shares an insightful proverb: as iron sharpens iron, so one person sharpens another (Proverbs 27:17). That is perfectly indicative of the relationship the two of us have—and of the relationship Black mothers can have with one another as they take the principles shared in this chapter of *Anatomy of a Black Mother* and apply them.

There are several areas where we feel that most of the Black mothers that we serve are *already* wise, even if they may not recognize it. A lot of our mothers don't give themselves credit for their uncanny ability to make a decision on a dime, or on a shoe-string, about their families, their kids, and how they are going to survive and thrive in a world that beats them up on a daily basis. They also don't realize that they intuitively know how to take challenges and turn them into opportunities. We have watched many of our mothers do that very thing. One mother thought she had failed miserably when it came to what was going on when her son was being bullied, but she had the wisdom to reach out to Black Mothers Forum and others for help and perspective. She eventually discovered that she had made a great decision for both her son and for herself.

Our mothers also have an innate bent toward common sense. Truth is, common sense isn't so common, but when they have to figure out how they are going to navigate work, home, and church or community with how their children are doing each and every day, common sense naturally comes into play. For example, if our child is sick and medicine is not an option because of financial limitations, we've learned from generation to generation that honey with lemon will soothe the throat. That is just one way that common sense becomes common.

Many of our mothers don't believe that they are good at handling their finances, yet we've seen women from generation to generation show how to take a dollar and stretch it. Our mothers can create something out of nothing. They can take beans and a peanut butter and jelly sandwich and make it seem like a gourmet meal. They are still paying their rent. Their children are still showing up for school because their children's education is very important to our mothers. They will do whatever it takes to make sure their children get to school, regardless of whether or not the school is mistreating them. We have witnessed many moms sacrifice so that their children could go to college. They have tremendous stories of working very hard and using much wisdom to put three or four children through college on a $30,000-a-year income.

There are three main areas, however, where we've found that most of the women that we serve can become *wiser*. The first is in their relationships with one another. We need to give ourselves more opportunity to intentionally set aside time to get to know other people outside of the realm of the stressors we are experiencing. Yet establishing such relationships can sometimes be difficult because just as trust is earned, distrust is learned. To make ourselves vulnerable is both a challenge and an opportunity. There are so many layers we have to unpeel to get to the heart of an individual woman.

Debora has observed what she calls the trilogy of female relationships, meaning that when three women come together, there is always that one who may feel more like an outsider. This trilogy works, though, when we go about identifying how we want our relationships to work and we become able to express our love for one another openly, without being hypercritical of one another in a way that brings someone down. Debora tells women, "You are not going to have 50 million best friends, so with the best friends you do have, you want to realize *why* they are your best friends. You have to nurture those relationships and be able to understand what makes those relationships important."

How is it that the mothers in Black Mothers Forum get along so well? What is it that gives us the love we have for one another that brings us excitement when we see each other and makes us want to celebrate one another? We've made it a point to edify and build up each other. We were intentional in the way we structured our guiding principles with that in mind. We listen to one another and do not attack each other, even though we may have different ideas, backgrounds, and perspectives. We look alike, but we understand that we come from varying socioeconomic, geographical, and educational backgrounds and possess different legacies, yet we bring all of that into the same space.

It's interesting when we see mothers come into the group. They watch us model out our love for one another and the intentionality we exhibit by building up each other. We get torn down all the time as women, yet people in the community respect us for how we interact with one another and work together to see what we can do to turn things around. We also build a safe environment for women to be themselves. I think of one Black Mothers Forum member, the youngest on our core team. Her colorful hair was indicative of how different her mindset was from the older mothers in the group, but when we were receptive to receive her and her ideas, she felt that love as we welcomed her as her authentic, colorful self.

In the journey of relationships, we have to know how to give and receive love, affection, and affirmation. Relationships are complex and vast, and we have to balance them all. Yet relationships are also beautiful, and we cannot exist on this earth without one another. It is people that make the world go around. Essential to this is knowing our worth and feeling worthy enough to have people in our lives who are worthy of us. If someone is going to be in our company, we must set the expectation to be treated according to our true self-worth and value. We come from Africa. We descend from a line of kings and queens. We are royalty and should be treated as such. Therefore, we must care about ourselves enough to recognize when a relationship (especially one with a significant other) may need to move to a different place or totally change.

That is the intersection between relationships and the next area where increased wisdom is needed: self-care. Some of our mothers lack in self-care. They find themselves overweight or not happy with the way they look in the mirror, so they don't want to receive themselves. The media has done such a disservice to women all over the world. We have tried to align our bodies and our looks to what we see on the screen, not operating in the reality that we are all unique individuals. Our bodies are going to be shaped differently because God created us that way. We need to be able to receive and accept ourselves for how we were formed in our mother's womb and what that looks like as we grow older. After all, when we look at our families, we have our own sisters from the same womb who come in multiple shapes.

> We are here by divine right, and we are beautiful, capable women.

It is so important that what we see of ourselves tells us that we are enough. We are here by divine right, and we are beautiful, capable women.

It is okay to embrace our complexity and to be who we are. In fact, another part of self-care involves researching and defining who we really are. As Black women, we need to take the time for self-discovery, to know our history and where we come from deep in Africa. Who were our ancestors, how did they get over here, and how did they make it through? We've heard some of our young people say they don't care about all of that. They know they are Black and about the Civil Rights Movement, but they are not interested in their own generational history and identity. That's a shame. For example, Debora's name is Debora Ruth. Her name was intentional, and she knows the story behind it. Both names are derived from the Bible. Deborah was a judge and a strong leader for her people. Ruth was a widow who cared so deeply for her mother-in-law, Naomi, that she left her own people to live with her and adopt Naomi's faith as her own. The name Debora Ruth means something significant and speaks to the legacy her parents intended for her.

We had a mother in Black Mothers Forum who presented herself in a way that showed she didn't want anyone to bother her. She wanted to portray herself as being a tough, rough-and-tumble woman. As a result, people didn't approach her. Yet Janelle saw her for who she really was. Janelle had to enter into her space, ask her some tough questions, and show her some things to break down that hard exterior—but within 15 minutes of their first meeting, the woman was amazed because no one had ever done that with her before. In time, the woman made some positive decisions that have been life changing for her and her children. She had tried to care for herself by creating a persona that she wanted others to see, but it didn't reflect who she truly was. It is when we find our authentic selves that we begin to feel good about and love ourselves. That positions us to better care for ourselves, and it makes it easier to step outside of ourselves to love and care for others.

Finally, we've discovered that our mothers need to have more wisdom when it comes to money management. As we mentioned earlier, most mothers do better at this than they think, but they still need to improve when it comes to how they spend their money, how they receive their money, and how they direct their money. Money is all about worth.

We challenge Black women to ask themselves, "What is my net worth?" "What am I worthy of?" If we are feeling powerless, what better way to make ourselves think we have power than to go out and get whatever we want even though we know we can't afford it? We tell ourselves, "Why shouldn't I have it?" instead of knowing that, yes, we do deserve the best, but there is work and responsibility that comes with having the money it takes to buy the best. There is work to be done, and it starts with us.

Another great question to ask is whether or not the thing we want is really going to make us feel great about ourselves. "Do I want it because it is going to make me look good?" "Do I want it because it is going to make me feel good?" "Do I want it because it is going to serve something in me to make me feel elevated?" "Do I need this, or do I *want* it?" Our answers to all of these questions will go a long way in helping us better manage our money.

—————

Of course, wisdom truly becomes a wise counselor only as much as we allow it to do so. As we've worked together over the years, Debora has tried to be a big sister to Janelle while, at the same time, being a partner and a friend who is walking in the same space for the same purpose and cause. We ask each other questions, including those we may not want to grapple with at the moment but know need to be discussed. That helps us to identify where we are in the moment compared to where we want to be. Janelle is a visionary in terms of wanting to see the future and the steps that go with it, so Debora strives to have those conversations with Janelle that will have the greatest impact.

Likewise, Debora says, there are times "when we can do the yin-yang flip where she needs to calm me down, and I need to calm her down because of the passion we feel for the people we are working with." These include students, educators, family and friends, and others in the community. Sometimes, we have to care for people much more than they care about themselves. That means we have to counsel one another to step back so that we don't feel we are being taken advantage of.

We have also learned how to easily forgive each other when we know the other person is in a stressful time so we can feel safe and have those breakthrough "aha" moments. Though we are exposed to a lot and know much, there are still things we don't know. Yet we are both avid learners, so not being afraid to learn from one another is important. We hope we show an example of how a multi-generational friendship and team partnership can work where we know when to lead and when to follow.

When it comes to providing wise counsel to Black mothers, Janelle likes to start with the question, "Why are you here today? What brought you to this point where you are now seeking me out?" One of the common areas where we've had to counsel mothers is on taking ownership and responsibility. We believe it is a wise thing to stop looking outside of ourselves and blaming everyone else for our circumstances. When we are wise, we understand ourselves and have a true assessment of who we really are and the roles we play in the situations we face. This positions us to put together some actionable items to move forward. Then, as Debora often says, they can start to go on a journey toward their own resolution. "It is about being self-aware," Debora says, "and turning that mirror inward to discover what and who you are, and if you've gone through something, who and what hurt you. What do you need to heal so you can go forward?"

We have also discovered that there is great value in spending time with older Black women and getting them to share their insights with the younger women. It is great to be able to glean from their years of experience and ask them thought-provoking questions to better understand why they believe what they believe. For example, some older mothers have a different perception of many of the systems that we are dealing with, such as education, because of how they were raised in those systems.

Because we have all come from different time periods, demographics, socioeconomics, and educational backgrounds, teaching younger mothers to listen carefully and not jump to conclusions is important. That way, they can shift their paradigm and see issues in a new light.

Interestingly, Debora says, "I like to ask women, 'Talk to me about your eight-year-old self.' At age eight, we are really starting to remember most things. It is fascinating when they start to connect with themselves and become aware of everything that was going on around them from a sensory standpoint, all the way to what might have been cooking in the kitchen or their favorite time of the year."

> Wisdom is often manifested in how we conduct ourselves on a daily basis and in different situations.

We counsel women to take time to step back, think about their lives, and realize that the pain they encountered can never be erased—but if they don't deal with it, it will erode their mental and physical health. We've also discovered that a lot of things start coming to light for women when they are in their forties. It makes sense. Many have gone through their childbearing years by then, years that are a blur for most women. As they did the best they could and poured their whole selves into their families, they lost sight of themselves.

Wisdom is often manifested in how we conduct ourselves on a daily basis and in different situations. Oftentimes, we don't have to speak. People are watching our actions. They speak volumes to other women even more than when we talk to them and ask them questions. In addition, wisdom comes in learning how to master our emotions to use them when we need to do so. If we need to shed a tear, we can control when to shed that tear. If we need to have righteous indignation, we know when to express it and how to say it.

Finally, we've seen that no woman wants to receive advice until they ask for it. True counsel occurs when someone is actually ready to receive it. It all goes back to self-awareness. We have to get to a place in our lives where we recognize we need wise counsel and someone to direct us.

———

In the end, it is important for all Black mothers to get involved in a cause. "Find something to take the light away from yourself," Debora said, "and maybe even from what you may be experiencing." It is also vital to be others focused. "When you are others focused, that requires a willingness to be present for someone else," Janelle said. "In turn, that individual then needs to want to turn around, pay it forward, and be there for others."

We believe there are two great things that wise counseling Black mothers can accomplish on a regular basis for their children, their families, and each other. First is consistency. We must be a role model, demonstrating the things we are speaking to others. We must always show up when we need to show up. We are always going to be present. We are steady and reliable. Sadly, too many young women tell us, "My mother may seem that way to you, but if you really knew her, you'd see why I don't respect her." That's unfortunate. Children are always looking for that adult who is going to be consistent.

Second is learning. It's true that sometimes we don't know what we don't know until something happens that triggers the need to learn. However, if we are striving for knowledge in the first place, that helps us to seek to understand how others feel and how they are navigating life so that we can set a personal standard for ourselves regardless of our past experiences. We want to get to the point where we can say, "I know that I can do whatever I set my mind to."

When we think about *Anatomy of a Black Mother*, the term "anatomy" encompasses both the internal and external workings of what is happening with us at home, at work, and in society. If we are able to set some foundations and expectations for ourselves, then we can start to understand the complexity of this reality called motherhood—and that is a great place to be!

KNOW WHO YOU ARE:
and Keep Standing!

"Many women do noble things, but you surpass them all."
~ Proverbs 31:29

As Black mothers, perseverance is always at the forefront of everything that we say and do on a daily basis. It is this ability to overcome the daily barriers thrown in our path that has equipped us to keep our eye on the prize. Our community continues to be upheld based on the love of a Black mother.

Yet it is because of those barriers, whether they be emotional or institutional, that we often have to reengage in a particular incident or situation because we were not given the opportunity to get it resolved the first time around. It is this drive to complete what we started, despite the challenges or opposition we face, which produces one of the strongest characteristics we possess as Black mothers—perseverance.

Biblically, perseverance is about having the endurance and the patience to do something while finding the mental strength to strive onward through any obstacles and setbacks. As we "run with perseverance the race marked out for us" (Hebrews 12:1) we develop our character and gain a renewed hope (Romans 5:4).

In the end, we are still standing.

In our work through Black Mothers Forum, I recall a situation where one of our ninth-grade Black sons had been suspended for allegedly leaving class without a hall pass and disrespecting the school security guard. He had already missed 10 days of school for a previous alleged incident of disrespect to another school official. School administrators repeatedly told his parents that he could not return until a certain date which would've kept him away from class for nearly 20 consecutive days. His mother would not give up. She had the strength to reach out to others like Black Mothers Forum to help her advocate for her son's return to school.

Guess what happened? When the community came to her support, the suspension was reversed. The child was reinstated and was even provided a tutor to help him catch up on the schoolwork he missed. Despite all the difficulties, she persevered, and we were able to make sure her son had what he needed to be academically successful. As a result of perseverance, he finished the school year with a higher grade point average than when he started, and he was free to go on to the next grade level with a clean disciplinary record because we were successful in getting his prior infractions removed.

A persevering mother possesses certain traits that enable her to overcome even the most egregious obstacles. First, she fully understands the reason why she is engaged in her pursuit. In other words, she knows her purpose. She understands why she must persevere. When our "why" is clear, that provides all the strength we need to press on. For most of us, our big "why" is simple. We want our children to be all that they were birthed to be so they can flourish in their talents and excel in their intelligence free from barriers.

We don't want their lives to be in jeopardy.

We don't want their educational endeavors to be in danger.

We just want them to live and thrive.

The next trait a persevering mother exhibits is the desire to do whatever it takes to reach the outcome she wants. This desire far outweighs any obstacles that try to keep her from achieving her goals. A mother with desire is not easily swayed or deterred from realizing her goal. She takes the initiative and needs no one to push or prod her to keep moving forward. She will remain unrelenting and unstoppable.

Attempt to get in her way if you dare. You may walk away with your ego a little bruised and some hurt feelings, but you will get the point and be willing to do whatever is necessary to help her accomplish her goals. If not, there will be no rest for anyone until she is satisfied that everything possible has been done to remedy her concern.

The third trait is a deep self-belief that we inherited from our foremothers. It reminds us, "I am somebody. I am human. I am worthy. I am of great value." We know that our foremothers were able to persevere and overcome the barriers of enslavement, Jim Crow laws, and segregation because they believed deeply that they were somebody. It is this self-belief that today's Black mother brings to the table, and it the same self-belief that declares, "I am worthy, therefore my children are worthy, too. They should be afforded the same opportunities as everyone else's children in this country."

The final trait of a persevering mother is a willpower that says, "You know what? I don't care what I have to set aside or what I have to sacrifice. If I have to go to work for 12 hours a day, come home, cook, clean, and help with homework, I'm going to do whatever it takes to make sure my child has a better life than I had." This willpower grants us the ability to delay our own gratification, override any unwelcome thoughts of giving up, and remain cool in the midst of the crazy crises that go on around us—knowing it is about more than us. We will make sure we put our children first. Sometimes that attitude can be detrimental if we get so bogged down that our mental health is challenged. That's when we must also have the willpower to take a break. If we don't, the break will take us.

> Our fortitude as Black mothers to persevere is not ideological. It is a reality.

Our fortitude as Black mothers to persevere is not ideological. It is not a concept. It is not a theory. It is a reality. I once worked with a mother who had two little children, lost her housing, and was unable to find new accommodations—so she went from pillar to post trying to find a way for her children to make it and still make sure they were in school. Oftentimes, because of the color of our skin or the way we enter into a space, people are reluctant to assist us. I've helped other Black mothers who were in abusive relationships get out while they could. Sadly, when we as Black mothers deal with domestic violence, it is often not taken as seriously as when our White sisters encounter the same thing. The violence done to us is seen as being deserved or as being less detrimental, or harmful, because we look tough and should be able to handle it. No one has ever taken a look at the toll domestic violence or abuse of any kind has had on Black women. This, too, is our reality.

———

I hope that you have found *Anatomy of a Black Mother* to be a beautifully woven tapestry of stories that exhibit the characteristics that make us who we are and who we want to be. By no means was I able to cover all the characteristics we possess in one book. It would take several books and many more stories about our brilliance, creativity, adaptability, power, and will to survive to do so.

My charge to you as we leave our time together is to be Black, bold, beautiful, and strong, and know that you are a Black mother—the earth's backbone.

ABOUT THE CONTRIBUTORS

Felisha Taylor—Felisha Taylor is an Arizona native, where she currently lives with her spouse, three children, and their dog. When she isn't working in the healthcare field, she enjoys spending quality time with her family, cooking, and helping others in the community.

Janice Varnado—Janice Varnado is a wife, mother, and advocate. Janice serves on the Black Mothers Forum governing board, Phoenix Human Relations Commission, and Head Start Birth to Five Policy Council. Janice is passionate about advocating for children and driven by her favorite quotes, "Service is the rent we pay to live on this earth," Shirley Chisholm, and "Education is the most powerful weapon which you can use to change the world," Nelson Mandela.

Debora R. Colbert-Green, AIM, AU, CTT+ CPC, PCC, PMP, MAOM—Visionary. Passionate. Innovator. As the Executive Director of Black Mothers Forum (2017) and The Black Mothers Forum Microschools (2021), Deb has been devoted to transformation of learning experiences for learners of all ages for decades. Known for mentoring, coaching, innovative thinking, and inspiring others, she collaborates with various school districts, universities, organizations, community leaders, students, and legislators to facilitate, design, and review educational initiatives, curriculum performance, policies, and procedures.

Deb's contribution to *Anatomy of a Black Mother* was based on her experiences and insight into the hearts and minds of others by listening to and feeling their heartfelt expressions and how important it is to have people in our lives as mothers, friends, and confidants that care and support us in our growth, personally and professionally, to dissect our decisions and suture our wounds as we take the journey of life. Relationships can be complicated, and are also the heartbeat, the breath, and blood flow that makes us who we are today!

Gwendolyn Payton—Gwendolyn Payton is a mother, grandmother, advocate, and minister. Gwendolyn is a charter member of the Black Mothers Forum, serves on their governing board, and is a microschool learning guide and Celebrate Recovery Leader for her church. Gwendolyn believes all children have a right to fulfill their hopes and dreams.

For more information about
Black Mothers Forum, visit
www.blackmothersforums.com

Scan to contact us:

Made in the USA
Monee, IL
07 July 2026

56553279R00100